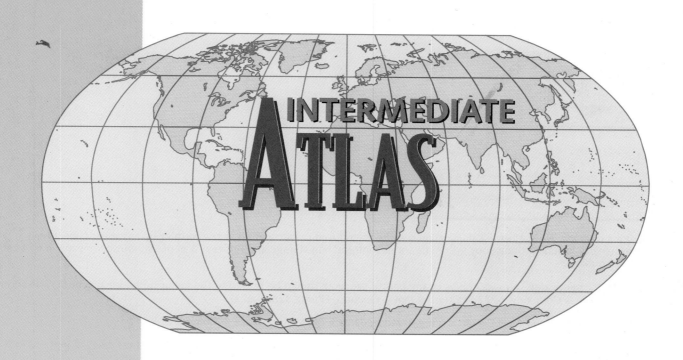

INTERMEDIATE ATLAS

HARCOURT BRACE & COMPANY

Orlando Atlanta Austin Boston San Francisco Chicago Dallas

New York Toronto London

 Visit The Learning Site at http://www.hbschool.com

Grateful acknowledgment is made to University of Missouri-Kansas City, University Libraries for permission to reprint "Maps" by Dorothy Brown Thompson.

Photo Credits:
Key: (t) top; (b) bottom; (l) left; (r) right; (c) center

5 John Henley; 5 (insets) Harcourt Brace and Company/Victoria Bowen; 66 Roy Morsch/The Stock Market; 67 (l) The Bettmann Archive; 67 (r) Pete Saloutos/The Stock Market; 70 (l) Jonathan Nourok/PhotoEdit; 70 (inset) David Young-Wolff/PhotoEdit; 70 (r) John Elk III/Stock Boston; 71 (l) Chuck O'Rear/Westlight; 71 (c) Doris De Witt/Tony Stone Images; 71 (r) Douglas A. Faulkner/Photo Researchers; 74 (l) Culver Pictures; 74 (inset) Lawrence Migdale/Stock, Boston; 74 (c), 74(r) Missouri Historical Society; 75 (l) Kansas State Historical Society; 75 (r) The Granger Collection, New York; 78 (l) E.R. Degginger/Color-Pic; 78 (inset) Willard Clay/Tony Stone Images; 78 (r) Richard Pasley/Stock, Boston; 79 (l) Mark Burnett/Photo Researchers; 79 (r) Jim Pickerell/Westlight; 82 (tl), 82(bl) Harcourt Brace & Company/Carroll Morgan; 82 (r) Greg Vaughan/Tom Stack & Associates; 83 (l) William S. Helsel/Tony Stone Images; 83 (c) Thomas H. Brakefield/The Stock Market; 83 (r) Vince Streano/The Stock Market.

All maps by GeoSystems

Printed in the United States of America

ISBN 0-15-310435-X

11 12 13 14   085   04 03 02

CONTENTS

Maps

by Dorothy Brown Thompson

High adventure
  And bright dream—
Maps are mightier
  Than they seem:

Ships that follow
  Leaning stars—
Red and gold of
  Strange bazaars—

Ice floes hid
  Beyond all knowing—
Planes that ride where
  Winds are blowing!

Train maps, maps of
  Wind and weather,
Road maps—taken
  Altogether

Maps are really
  Magic wands
For home-staying
  Vagabonds!

Read a Map

Why Is This Skill Important?

To answer questions about the world around you, you need information. You can get this information by reading this atlas, by looking at its pictures and charts, and by studying its maps. Maps tell you about the five themes of geography—location, place, human-environment interactions, movement, and regions. Knowing how to read maps is an important skill both for learning social studies and for taking action as a citizen.

The Parts of a Map

Most maps have several things in common. To help you read maps, mapmakers usually include a title, a key, a compass rose, a locator, and a scale on the maps they draw.

The map title tells you the subject of the map. Look the map below. What is the title of this map?

The map title may also help you understand what kind of map is shown. There are many kinds of maps. One kind is a physical map. It

THE UNITED STATES

RUSSIA
ARCTIC OCEAN
ALASKA   CANADA
Juneau
0 200 400 Miles
0 400 Kilometers
PACIFIC OCEAN

National capital
★ State capital
National border
State border

CANADA

0 200 400 Miles
0 200 400 Kilometers
Albers Equal-Area Projection

Olympia
WA
Salem
OR
ID
★ Boise
Helena
MT
ND
★ Bismarck
SD
★ Pierre
WY
Cheyenne
MN
St. Paul
Lake Superior
Lake Michigan
Lake Huron
WI
Madison
MI
Lansing
Lake Ontario
Lake Erie
NH   ME
Augusta
Montpelier ★
VT
NY
Albany ★
Concord
Boston
MA
Hartford ★
Providence
RI
CT
PA
Harrisburg ★
NJ
★ Trenton
Sacramento
Carson City ★
NV
Salt Lake City ★
UT
Denver ★
CO
NE
Lincoln ★
IA
Des Moines ★
IL
Indianapolis ★
IN
Columbus ★
OH
Dover
MD
DE
Annapolis
Washington, D.C.
WV
Charleston ★
VA
Richmond
CA
AZ
★ Phoenix
Santa Fe ★
NM
Topeka ★
KS
MO
Jefferson City ★
Springfield
Frankfort ★
KY
Nashville ★
TN
NC
Raleigh
Columbia
SC
ATLANTIC OCEAN
PACIFIC OCEAN
OK
Oklahoma City ★
AR
Little Rock ★
AL
★ Atlanta
GA
MS
Jackson ★
Montgomery ★
LA
Baton Rouge ★
TX
Austin ★
Tallahassee ★
FL
HAWAII
★ Honolulu
0 100 Miles
0 100 Kilometers
PACIFIC OCEAN
MEXICO
Gulf of Mexico
N
W   E
S

shows mostly landforms and bodies of water. Another kind of map is a political map. It shows mostly cities and state or national boundaries. **Boundary** is another word for *border,* or the outside edge of a place. What two countries share a national border with the United States?

⊛ National capital

★ State capital

━━━ National border

─── State border

The **map key**, which is sometimes called a map legend, explains what the symbols on the map stand for. A **symbol** is something that stands for something else. On a map, a symbol represents a real object in the world. Symbols on maps may be colors, patterns, lines, or other special marks. On the map on page 6, a star is used to show a state capital. What symbol is used to show the national capital?

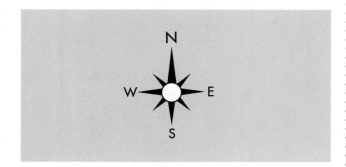

The **compass rose**, or direction marker on a map, shows the main directions, or cardinal directions. The **cardinal directions** are north, south, east, and west. The compass rose also helps you find the **intermediate directions**, or the directions between the cardinal directions. Intermediate directions are northeast, southeast, southwest, and northwest.

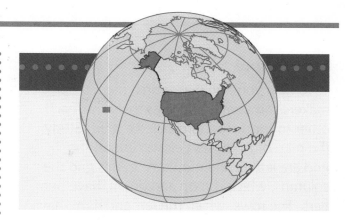

The **locator** is a small map or globe that shows where the place on the main map is located in a state, in a country, or in the world. The locator on the map of the United States is a globe that shows North America. The United States is shown in red.

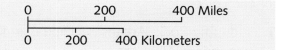

The **map scale** compares a distance on a map with a distance in the real world. A map scale helps you find the real distance between places on a map. Each map in this atlas has a scale that shows both miles and kilometers.

Find Alaska and Hawaii on the map of the United States. These states are not shown where they really are. Hundreds of miles separate them from the other 48 states. To show the whole area between Alaska, Hawaii, and the other states, the map would have to be much larger, or each part of the map would have to be much smaller. Instead, Alaska and Hawaii are each shown in an **inset map**, or a small map within a larger map. The boxes around Alaska and Hawaii show that they are inset maps.

An inset map often has its own map scale. Look at Alaska on the map of the United States. On the Earth, Alaska is more than twice the size of Texas, but on the map, Alaska is much smaller than Texas. This is because the scales on the inset map and the main map are different.

Understand the Process

To help you find places on a map, map-makers sometimes add lines that cross each other to form a pattern called a **grid**. Study the map of Arkansas below. Around the grid are letters and numbers. In this grid the columns, which run up and down, have numbers. The rows, which run left and right, have letters. Each square on the map can be identified by its letter and number.

A map with a grid may have an index such as the one you see beside this map. The index helps you find the names of the places you are looking for. It lists them in alphabetical order. The index also gives the grid letter and number for each place.

1. Find Little Rock, Arkansas's capital, in the map index. What are Little Rock's grid letter and number?

2. Find the letter *B* and the number *2* on the grid. Put a finger of one hand on the letter *B* and a finger of your other hand on the number *2*. Move your fingers toward each other, along row B and column 2. You will find Little Rock in the square where your fingers meet.

3. Now find Fayetteville on the map. In what square is it located? In what square is the city of Fort Smith located?

4. What city is located in square *C-3*? Check your answer with the map index.

Think and Apply

Look at the map of Arkansas again. Identify the parts of the map, and discuss with a partner what the map tells you about the state. Then take turns using the map grid to find different places in the state.

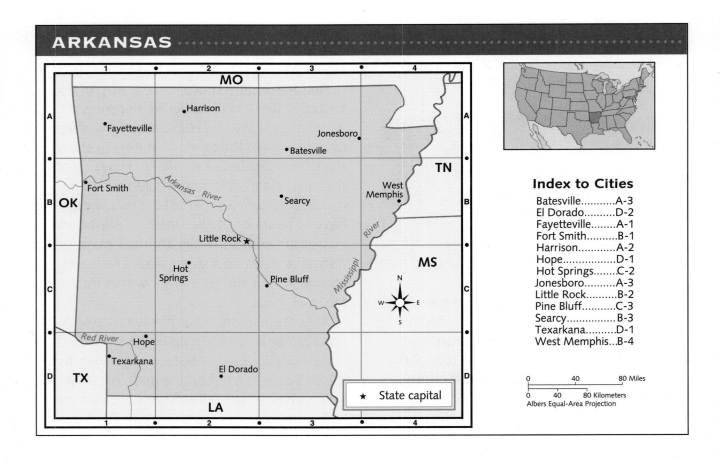

ARKANSAS

Index to Cities

Batesville...........A-3
El Dorado..........D-2
Fayetteville........A-1
Fort Smith.........B-1
Harrison............A-2
Hope.................D-1
Hot Springs........C-2
Jonesboro..........A-3
Little Rock..........B-2
Pine Bluff..........C-3
Searcy................B-3
Texarkana.........D-1
West Memphis...B-4

0   40   80 Miles
0   40   80 Kilometers
Albers Equal-Area Projection

Use Latitude and Longitude

Why Is This Skill Important?

Just as the numbers of your home address describe where you live in your town, the numbers of your global address tell where your town is located on the Earth. The numbers in a global address stand for lines of latitude and lines of longitude. You can use these lines to help you describe the absolute, or exact, location of any place on the Earth.

Lines of Latitude

Mapmakers use a system of imaginary lines to form a grid on maps and globes. The lines that run east and west are the **lines of latitude**. Lines of latitude are also called **parallels** (PAIR•uh•lelz). This is because they are parallel, or always the same distance from each other. Parallel lines never meet.

Lines of latitude are measured in degrees north and south from the equator, which is

labeled 0°, or *zero degrees*. The parallels north of the equator are marked *N* for *north latitude*. This means they are in the Northern Hemisphere. The parallels south of the equator are marked *S* for *south latitude*. This means they are in the Southern Hemisphere. The greater the number of degrees marking a parallel, the farther north or south of the equator it is.

Lines of Longitude

The lines that run north and south on a map are the **lines of longitude**, or **meridians**. Each meridian runs from the North Pole to the South Pole. Unlike parallels, which never meet, meridians meet at the poles. Meridians are farthest apart at the equator.

Meridians are numbered in much the same way as parallels are numbered. The meridian marked 0° is called the **prime meridian**. It runs north and south through Greenwich, near the

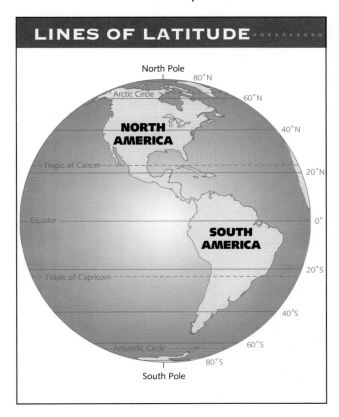

LINES OF LATITUDE

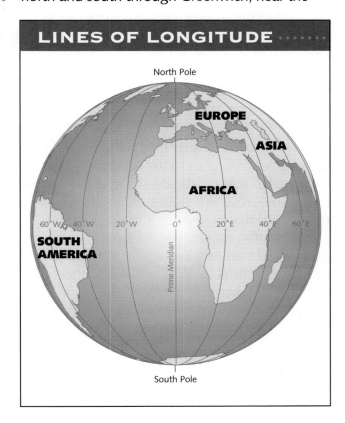

LINES OF LONGITUDE

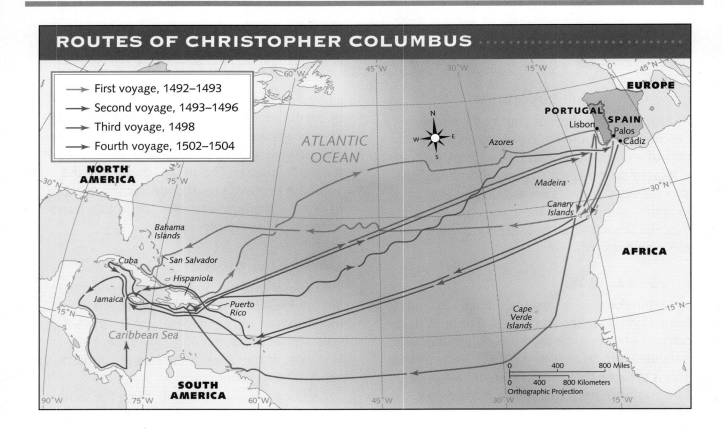

ROUTES OF CHRISTOPHER COLUMBUS

Legend:
→ First voyage, 1492–1493
→ Second voyage, 1493–1496
→ Third voyage, 1498
→ Fourth voyage, 1502–1504

NORTH AMERICA

ATLANTIC OCEAN

EUROPE

PORTUGAL
Lisbon

SPAIN
Palos
Cádiz

Azores

Madeira

Canary Islands

AFRICA

Bahama Islands

Cuba   San Salvador

Hispaniola

Jamaica

Puerto Rico

Caribbean Sea

Cape Verde Islands

SOUTH AMERICA

0   400   800 Miles
0   400   800 Kilometers
Orthographic Projection

---

city of London in Britain. Lines of longitude to the west of the prime meridian are marked *W* for *west longitude*. They are in the Western Hemisphere. The meridians to the east of prime meridian are marked *E* for *east longitude*. They are in the Eastern Hemisphere.

Understand the Process

The map above shows the four voyages of Christopher Columbus to the Americas. The map has a grid of lines of latitude and longitude drawn over it. The crossing lines of latitude and longitude make it possible to describe absolute location.

Like most maps, this one does not show every parallel and meridian. Every fifteenth parallel is shown from 15°N to 45°N, and every fifteenth meridian is shown from 0° to 90°W.

Now that you know about lines of latitude and longitude, you can use them to find some locations. At either side of the map, find 30°N. At the top or bottom, find 15°W. Use a finger of each hand to trace these lines to the point where they cross each other. The Canary Islands

are not far from this point. So you can say that the location of the Canary Islands is near 30°N, 15°W.

Look for the latitude and longitude that describe the location of Columbus's first landing in the Americas. The closest parallels are 15°N and 30°N. The closest meridian is 75°W. So you can say that the location of the first landing is about 22°N, 75°W.

Think and Apply

Think about what you just learned about latitude and longitude. Use the map to answer these questions.

1. What line of latitude is closest to Hispaniola?
2. What line of longitude is closest to the Bahama Islands?
3. What islands are located near 15°N, 30°W?
4. Which location is farther north, 45°N, 60°W or 30°N, 90°W?
5. Which location is farther east, 45°N, 60°W or 30°N, 90°W?

Compare Maps with Different Projections

Why Is This Skill Important?

Over the centuries Arab, Chinese, and European mapmakers have developed different ways to show the round Earth in the form of a flat map. These different representations of the Earth are called **projections**. Every map projection has **distortions**, or parts that are not accurate. This is because the shape of the round Earth needs to be split or stretched to make it flat. Identifying these distortions will help you understand how map projections can best be used.

Map Projections and Their Uses

Different kinds of map projections have different kinds of distortions. Some map projections distort the shape or the size of the area shown. Some show distances to be greater or less than they actually are. One way that mapmakers

classify map projections is by the properties that are distorted the least.

Map A is an equal-area projection. Notice that the prime meridian and the equator divide the hemispheres so that their areas are equal. An **equal-area projection** shows the sizes of regions in correct relation to one another, but it distorts shapes. Because an equal-area projection shows correct size relations of regions, it is useful for comparing information about different parts of the world. The projection on Map A below is just one of the many different kinds of equal-area projections.

Map B is a conformal projection. Notice that the lines of longitude are all an equal distance apart. On a globe the lines of longitude get closer together as they near the poles, where they meet. Also notice on Map B that the lines of latitude closer to the poles are farther apart.

MAP A: EQUAL-AREA PROJECTION

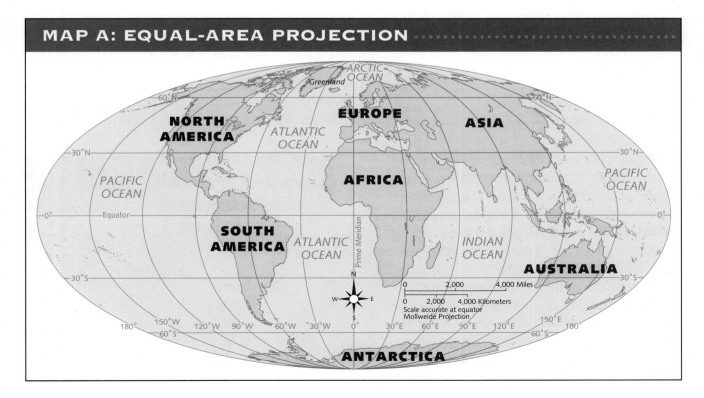

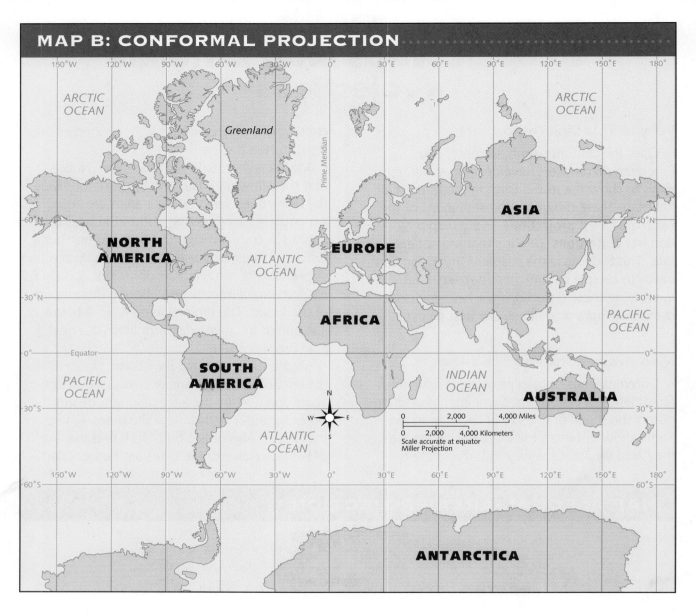

MAP B: CONFORMAL PROJECTION

ARCTIC OCEAN

Greenland

Prime Meridian

ARCTIC OCEAN

ASIA

NORTH AMERICA

EUROPE

ATLANTIC OCEAN

AFRICA

Equator

SOUTH AMERICA

PACIFIC OCEAN

INDIAN OCEAN

AUSTRALIA

PACIFIC OCEAN

ATLANTIC OCEAN

```
0          2,000        4,000 Miles
0     2,000      4,000 Kilometers
Scale accurate at equator
Miller Projection
```

ANTARCTICA

On a globe the lines of latitude are an equal distance apart. A **conformal projection** shows directions correctly, but it distorts sizes, especially of places near the poles. The Miller projection, shown above on Map B, is just one example of a conformal projection. Another that you may see is the Mercator (mer•KAY•ter) projection. Still another type of map, the Robinson projection, is a combination of equal-area and conformal projections. Map C is an example of a Robinson projection.

Map D is an **equidistant projection**. It shows accurate distances from a central point. Any

MAP C: ROBINSON PROJECTION

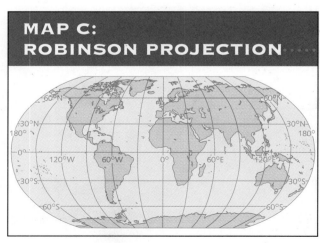

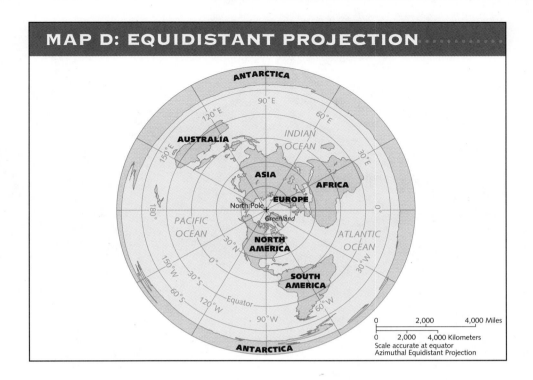

MAP D: EQUIDISTANT PROJECTION

ANTARCTICA

90°E

120°E

60°E

AUSTRALIA

INDIAN OCEAN

150°E

30°E

ASIA

AFRICA

180°

EUROPE

North Pole

0°

Greenland

PACIFIC OCEAN

ATLANTIC OCEAN

30°N

NORTH AMERICA

150°W

30°S

0°

SOUTH AMERICA

60°S

60°W

120°W

Equator

90°W

ANTARCTICA

| 0 | 2,000 | 4,000 Miles |
| 0 | 2,000 | 4,000 Kilometers |

Scale accurate at equator
Azimuthal Equidistant Projection

place on the Earth can be chosen as the central point. Often the central point chosen is one of the poles. That kind of map is called a **polar projection**. Either the North Pole or the South Pole can be the center of a polar projection. Notice on Map D that the North Pole is at the center of the map. The lines of latitude are circles, and the circles farther from the center are larger. Lines of longitude on Map D are straight lines that extend from the center in all directions, like the spokes of a wheel.

A **great circle** is any imaginary circle that divides the Earth into equal parts. The equator is a great circle. Lines of longitude are great circles, too. Because the Earth's surface is curved, the shortest distance between any two places is not really a straight line but part of a great circle. An equidistant projection is useful for finding the distance from the central point to other places on the map. Another projection, the gnomonic projection, is also important when studying great circle routes. In this projection all straight lines are great circle routes. Therefore, these lines show the shortest routes between two places. Distances on this projection are not accurate, however.

Understand the Process

Compare and contrast Maps A, B, C, and D by answering the questions below. As you answer the questions, think about the advantages and disadvantages of each map projection.

1. South America is much larger than Greenland. Which projection shows Greenland's size more accurately, Map A or Map B?
2. The greatest east-west distance in Africa is about the same as the greatest north-south distance. Which projection shows Africa's shape more accurately, Map A or Map B?
3. The North Pole is a single point. Which projections show the North Pole accurately?
4. Which map can be called a polar projection?
5. On which map do the lines of longitude get closer together toward both poles?
6. On which map or maps are the lines of longitude parallel, or equally far apart?

Think and Apply

Write a paragraph about the advantages and disadvantages of using each kind of map.

GEOGRAPHY TERMS

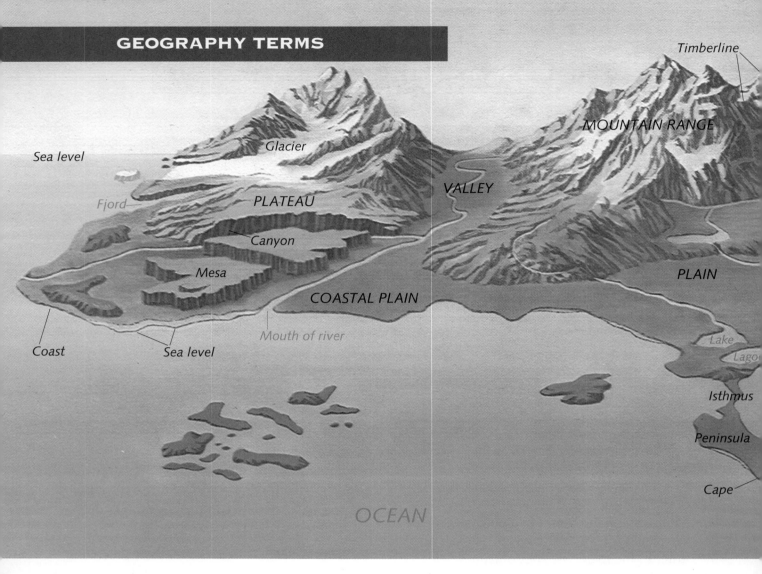

Timberline

MOUNTAIN RANGE

Sea level

Glacier

VALLEY

Fjord

PLATEAU

Canyon

PLAIN

Mesa

COASTAL PLAIN

Coast

Mouth of river

Sea level

Lake

Lagoon

Isthmus

Peninsula

Cape

OCEAN

basin bowl-shaped area of land surrounded by higher land

bay body of water that is part of a sea or ocean and is partly enclosed by land

bluff high, steep face of rock or earth

canyon deep, narrow valley with steep sides

cape a point of land that extends into water

cataract large waterfall

cliff high, steep face of rock or earth

coast land along a sea or ocean

coastal plain area of flat land along a sea or ocean

delta triangle-shaped area of land at the mouth of a river

desert dry land with few plants

dune hill of sand piled up by the wind

fall line area along which rivers form waterfalls or rapids as the rivers drop to lower land

fjord deep, narrow part of a sea or ocean, between high, steep banks

floodplain flat land that is near the edges of a river and is formed by the silt deposited by floods

foothills hilly area at the base of a mountain

glacier large ice mass that moves slowly down a mountain or across land

gulf body of water that is partly enclosed by land but is larger than a bay

hill land that rises above the land around it

island land that has water on all sides

isthmus narrow strip of land connecting two larger areas of land

lagoon body of shallow water

lake body of water with land on all sides

marsh lowland with moist soil and tall grasses

mesa flat-topped mountain with steep sides

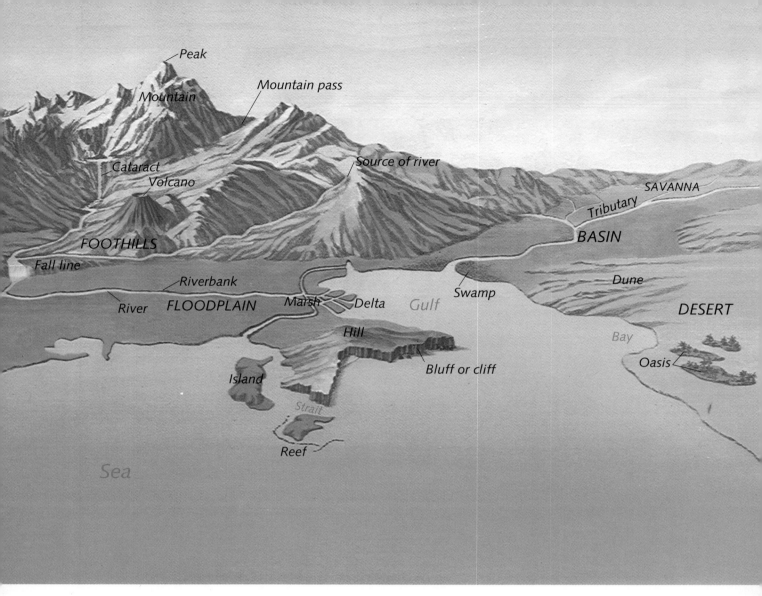

Peak

Mountain

Mountain pass

Source of river

SAVANNA

Cataract

Volcano

Tributary

BASIN

FOOTHILLS

Fall line

Riverbank

Dune

River

FLOODPLAIN

Marsh

Delta

Swamp

Gulf

DESERT

Hill

Bay

Bluff or cliff

Oasis

Island

Strait

Reef

Sea

mountain highest kind of land

mountain pass gap between mountains

mountain range row of mountains

mouth of river place where a river empties into another body of water

oasis area of water and fertile land with desert on all sides

ocean body of salt water, larger than a sea

peak top of a mountain

peninsula land that is almost completely surrounded by water

plain flat land

plateau area of high, flat land with steep sides

reef ridge of sand, rock, or coral that lies at or near the surface of a sea or ocean

river large stream of water that flows across the land

riverbank land along a river

savanna large area of grassland containing scattered trees

sea body of salt water, smaller than an ocean

sea level the level that is even with the surface of an ocean or sea

source of river place where a river or stream begins

strait narrow channel of water connecting two larger bodies of water

swamp area of low, wet land with trees

timberline line on a mountain above which it is too cold for trees to grow

tributary stream or river that empties into a larger river

valley low land between hills or mountains

volcano opening in the Earth, often raised, through which lava, rock, ashes, and gases are forced out

THE WORLD

THE WORLD: POLITICAL

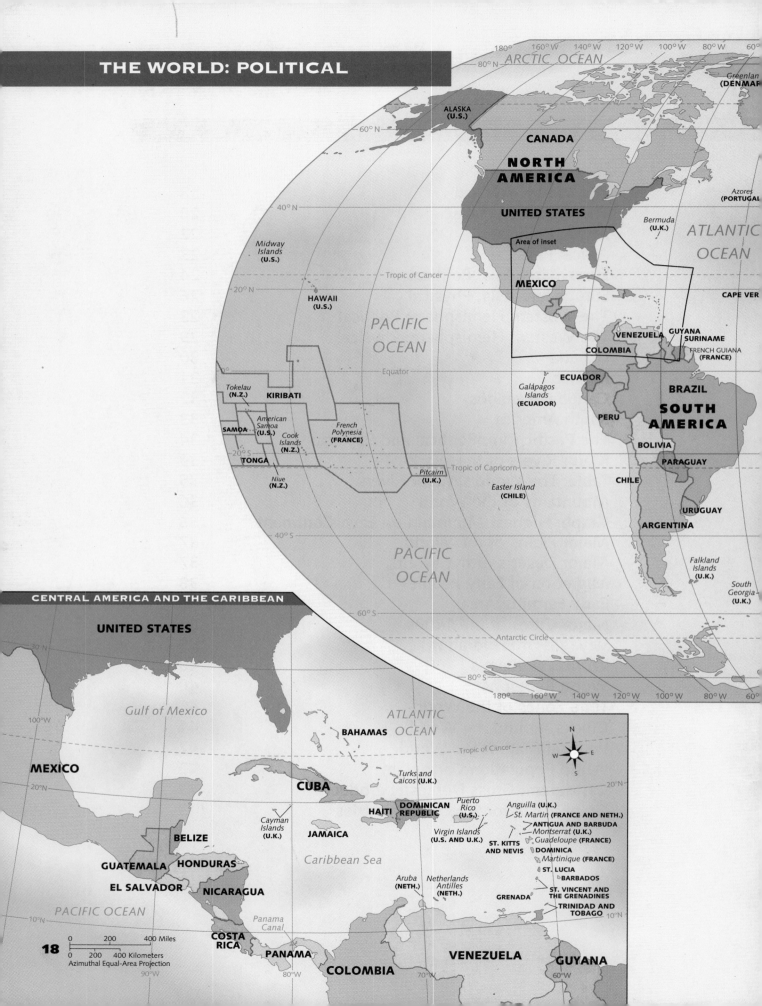

ARCTIC OCEAN

180° 160° W 140° W 120° W 100° W 80° 60°

80° N

Greenland
(DENMAR

ALASKA
(U.S.)

60° N

CANADA

**NORTH
AMERICA**

40° N

UNITED STATES

Bermuda
(U.K.)

Azores
(PORTUGAL

ATLANTIC
OCEAN

*Midway
Islands
(U.S.)*

20° N

Tropic of Cancer

Area of inset

CAPE VER

MEXICO

*HAWAII
(U.S.)*

**PACIFIC
OCEAN**

VENEZUELA

**GUYANA
SURINAME**

COLOMBIA

FRENCH GUIANA
(FRANCE)

Equator

*Galápagos
Islands
(ECUADOR)*

ECUADOR

*Tokelau
(N.Z.)*

KIRIBATI

BRAZIL

**SOUTH
AMERICA**

PERU

*American
Samoa
(U.S.)*

SAMOA

*Cook
Islands
(N.Z.)*

*French
Polynesia
(FRANCE)*

BOLIVIA

20° S

TONGA

*Niue
(N.Z.)*

*Pitcairn
(U.K.)*

Tropic of Capricorn

PARAGUAY

*Easter Island
(CHILE)*

CHILE

URUGUAY

40° S

ARGENTINA

PACIFIC
OCEAN

*Falkland
Islands
(U.K.)*

*South
Georgia
(U.K.)*

60° S

Antarctic Circle

80° S

180° 160° W 140° W 120° W 100° W 80° W 60°

UNITED STATES

20° N

Gulf of Mexico

ATLANTIC
OCEAN

BAHAMAS

100°W

Tropic of Cancer

N
W E
S

20°N

MEXICO

20°N

CUBA

*Turks and
Caicos (U.K.)*

Anguilla (U.K.)
St. Martin **(FRANCE AND NETH.)**
ANTIGUA AND BARBUDA
Montserrat **(U.K.)**
Guadeloupe **(FRANCE)**

**DOMINICAN
REPUBLIC**

*Puerto
Rico
(U.S.)*

HAITI

*Cayman
Islands
(U.K.)*

JAMAICA

BELIZE

*Virgin Islands
(U.S. AND U.K.)*

**ST. KITTS
AND NEVIS**

DOMINICA

Martinique **(FRANCE)**

ST. LUCIA

BARBADOS

Caribbean Sea

GUATEMALA

HONDURAS

*Aruba
(NETH.)*

*Netherlands
Antilles
(NETH.)*

**ST. VINCENT AND
THE GRENADINES**

EL SALVADOR

NICARAGUA

GRENADA

**TRINIDAD AND
TOBAGO**

10°N

PACIFIC OCEAN

*Panama
Canal*

10°N

18

0   200   400 Miles

0   200   400 Kilometers
Azimuthal Equal-Area Projection

**COSTA
RICA**

PANAMA

COLOMBIA

VENEZUELA

GUYANA

90°W

80°W

70°

60°W

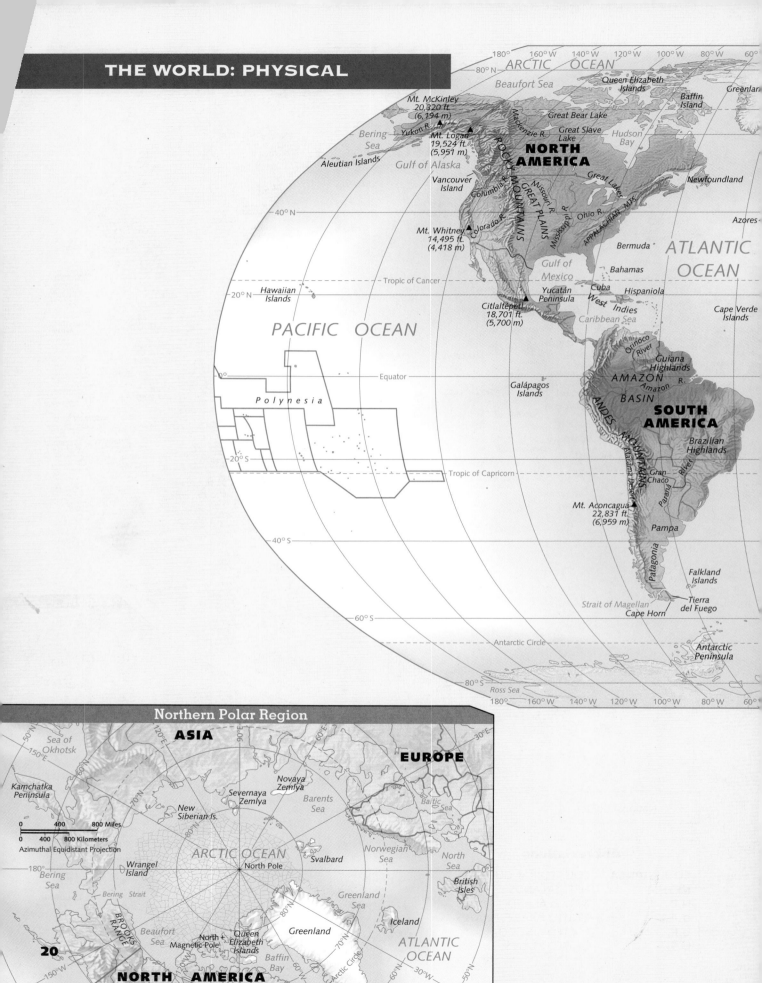

ARCTIC OCEAN
Beaufort Sea
Queen Elizabeth Islands
Greenland
Baffin Island
80° N

180° 160° W 140° W 120° W 100° W 80° W 60°

Bering Sea
Aleutian Islands
Gulf of Alaska

Mt. McKinley
20,320 ft.
(6,194 m)
Yukon R.
Mt. Logan
19,524 ft.
(5,951 m)

Mackenzie R.
Great Bear Lake
Great Slave Lake
Hudson Bay

NORTH AMERICA

ROCKY MOUNTAINS
Columbia R.
Vancouver Island

Great Lakes
Newfoundland

40° N

Mt. Whitney
14,495 ft.
(4,418 m)
Colorado R.
Missouri R.
GREAT PLAINS
Rio Grande
Ohio R.
Mississippi R.
APPALACHIAN MTS.

Azores

Tropic of Cancer

Bermuda
ATLANTIC OCEAN

20° N

Hawaiian Islands

Gulf of Mexico
Yucatán Peninsula
Bahamas
Cuba
West Indies
Hispaniola

Cape Verde Islands

PACIFIC OCEAN

Citlaltépetl
18,701 ft.
(5,700 m)
Caribbean Sea

0°
Equator

Galápagos Islands

Orinoco River
Guiana Highlands
AMAZON
Amazon R.
BASIN

Polynesia

SOUTH AMERICA

ANDES MOUNTAINS
Brazilian Highlands

20° S

Atacama Desert
Gran Chaco
Paraná River

Tropic of Capricorn

Mt. Aconcagua
22,831 ft.
(6,959 m)
Pampa

40° S

Patagonia
Falkland Islands

Strait of Magellan
Cape Horn
Tierra del Fuego

60° S

Antarctic Circle
Antarctic Peninsula

80° S
Ross Sea
180° 160° W 140° W 120° W 100° W 80° W 60°

Northern Polar Region

Sea of Okhotsk
ASIA
120° E
90° E
60° E
30° E
EUROPE

50° E
150° E

Kamchatka Peninsula
60° N
70° N
New Siberian Is.
Severnaya Zemlya
Novaya Zemlya
Barents Sea
Baltic Sea

0   400   800 Miles
0   400   800 Kilometers
Azimuthal Equidistant Projection

180°
Wrangel Island
ARCTIC OCEAN
North Pole
Svalbard
Norwegian Sea
North Sea

Bering Sea
Bering Strait

Greenland Sea
British Isles

BROOKS RANGE
Beaufort Sea
North Magnetic Pole
Queen Elizabeth Islands
Greenland
80° N
70° N
Iceland

20

Baffin Bay
Arctic Circle
60°
30° W
50°
ATLANTIC OCEAN

PACIFIC OCEAN
NORTH AMERICA
150° E

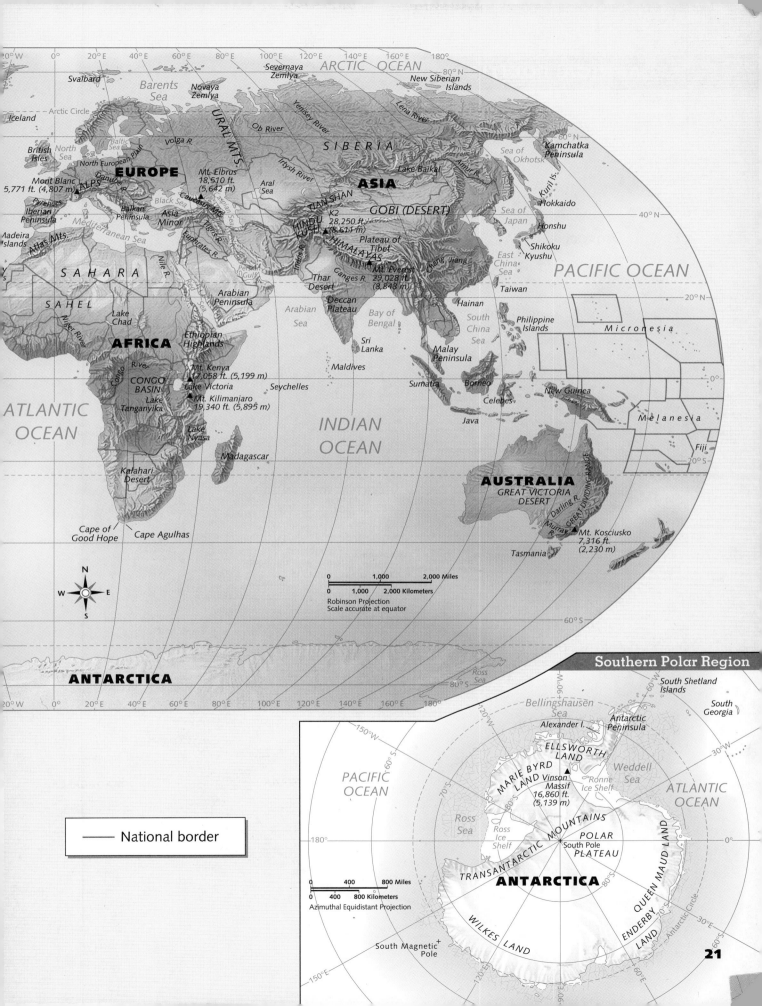

20°W 0° 20°E 40°E 60°E 80°E 100°E 120°E 140°E 160°E 180°

ARCTIC OCEAN

Svalbard
Barents Sea
Novaya Zemlya
Severnaya Zemlya
New Siberian Islands
80°N

Iceland
Arctic Circle
60°N

British Isles
North Sea
Baltic Sea
North European Plain
URAL MTS.
Ob River
Yenisey River
SIBERIA
Lena River
Kamchatka Peninsula
Sea of Okhotsk
Kuril Is.

EUROPE
Mt. Elbrus 18,510 ft. (5,642 m)
Volga R.
Irtysh River
Lake Baikal
Amur R.
Hokkaido
40°N

Mont Blanc 15,771 ft. (4,807 m)
ALPS
Danube R.
Black Sea
Caucasus Mts.
Caspian Sea
Aral Sea
TIAN SHAN
ASIA
K2 28,250 ft. (8,611 m)
GOBI (DESERT)
Honshu
Sea of Japan
Shikoku
Kyushu

Pyrenees
Iberian Peninsula
Balkan Peninsula
Asia Minor
Tigris R.
Euphrates R.
HINDU KUSH
HIMALAYAS
Plateau of Tibet
Mt. Everest 29,028 ft. (8,848 m)
Chang Jiang
East China Sea
Taiwan

Madeira Islands
Atlas Mts.
Mediterranean Sea
Nile R.
SAHARA
Persian Gulf
Thar Desert
Ganges R.
Deccan Plateau
Bay of Bengal
Hainan
20°N

SAHEL
Lake Chad
Arabian Peninsula
Arabian Sea
Sri Lanka
South China Sea
Philippine Islands
Micronesia

AFRICA
Niger River
Ethiopian Highlands
Mt. Kenya 17,058 ft. (5,199 m)
Maldives
Sumatra
Borneo
Malay Peninsula
New Guinea
0°

ATLANTIC OCEAN
Congo River
CONGO BASIN
Lake Victoria
Lake Tanganyika
Mt. Kilimanjaro 19,340 ft. (5,895 m)
Seychelles
INDIAN OCEAN
Java
Celebes
Melanesia
Fiji
20°S

Lake Nyasa
Madagascar
AUSTRALIA
GREAT VICTORIA DESERT
GREAT DIVIDING RANGE
Darling R.

Kalahari Desert
Murray R.
Mt. Kosciusko 7,316 ft. (2,230 m)

Cape of Good Hope
Cape Agulhas
Tasmania

N
W   E
S

0   1,000   2,000 Miles
0   1,000   2,000 Kilometers
Robinson Projection
Scale accurate at equator

60°S

ANTARCTICA
Ross Sea
80°S

20°W 0° 20°E 40°E 60°E 80°E 100°E 120°E 140°E 160°E 180°

——— National border

Southern Polar Region

Bellingshausen Sea
South Shetland Islands
South Georgia
Alexander I.
Antarctic Peninsula
ELLSWORTH LAND
30°W

PACIFIC OCEAN
60°S
MARIE BYRD LAND
Vinson Massif 16,860 ft. (5,139 m)
Ronne Ice Shelf
Weddell Sea
ATLANTIC OCEAN

180°
70°S
Ross Sea
Ross Ice Shelf
80°S
TRANSANTARCTIC MOUNTAINS
South Pole
POLAR PLATEAU
QUEEN MAUD LAND
0°

ANTARCTICA
WILKES LAND
ENDERBY LAND
Antarctic Circle
30°E

0   400   800 Miles
0   400   800 Kilometers
Azimuthal Equidistant Projection

South Magnetic Pole

150°E 120°E 60°E

21

AFRICA: POLITICAL

EUROPE

ASIA

ATLANTIC OCEAN

Mediterranean Sea

Madeira Islands (PORTUGAL)

Ceuta (SPAIN)
Algiers
Tunis
Tangier
Constantine
Rabat
Fès
Oran
Melilla (SPAIN)
Casablanca
Sfax
Marrakech
TUNISIA
Tripoli
MOROCCO
Banghazi

Canary Islands (SPAIN)

WESTERN SAHARA
(Occupied by Morocco)
El Aaiún

ALGERIA

LIBYA

EGYPT

Alexandria
Port Said
Tanta
Al Jizah
Suez
Cairo

Aswan

Tropic of Cancer

MAURITANIA

NIGER

CHAD

SUDAN

Port Sudan

Red Sea

Nouakchott

Timbuktu
MALI
Gao

Omdurman
Khartoum

ERITREA
Asmara

Gulf of Aden

Dakar
SENEGAL
Niamey

Bamako

N'Djamena

DJIBOUTI
Djibouti

GAMBIA
Banjul

BURKINA FASO
Ouagadougou

Kano

GUINEA-BISSAU
Bissau

BENIN

NIGERIA
Abuja

Lake Chad

Addis Ababa
Dire Dawa

GUINEA

Conakry
SIERRA LEONE
Freetown

CÔTE D'IVOIRE
GHANA
TOGO

Ogbomosho
Ibadan

CENTRAL AFRICAN REPUBLIC

ETHIOPIA

Monrovia
Yamoussoukro

Lomé
Lagos
Porto-Novo

Bangui

SOMALIA

LIBERIA
Abidjan
Accra

CAMEROON
Douala

Gulf of Guinea

Malabo

Yaoundé

UGANDA

KENYA

Mogadishu

EQUATORIAL GUINEA

Kisangani
Kampala
Kisumu

SAO TOME AND PRINCIPE

Libreville
GABON

Republic of the CONGO

Democratic Republic of CONGO

Nairobi
Kismaayo

0° Equator

São Tomé

RWANDA
Kigali

Lake Victoria

INDIAN OCEAN

Annobón (EQUATORIAL GUINEA)

Brazzaville
Kinshasa

Bujumbura
BURUNDI

Mwanza

Mombasa

Kananga

Dodoma

Ascension (UNITED KINGDOM)

ATLANTIC OCEAN

CABINDA (ANGOLA)

Mbuji-Mayi

Lake Tanganyika

TANZANIA

Dar es Salaam

Luanda

Kolwezi

Lubumbashi

COMOROS
Moroni

St. Helena (UNITED KINGDOM)

Lobito
ANGOLA
Huambo

Kitwe
ZAMBIA

Lake Malawi

MALAWI
Lilongwe

Blantyre

Lusaka

Harare

MOZAMBIQUE
Beira

Antananarivo

ZIMBABWE
Bulawayo

NAMIBIA

BOTSWANA

Windhoek

MADAGASCAR

Mozambique Channel

Tropic of Capricorn

Gaborone
Pretoria

Johannesburg
Mbabane
Maputo

SWAZILAND

Kimberley
Bloemfontein

Maseru
LESOTHO
Durban

SOUTH AFRICA

Cape Town

Port Elizabeth

N
W E
S

National border
National capital
Major city

0   500   1,000 Miles
0   500   1,000 Kilometers
Azimuthal Equal-Area Projection

22

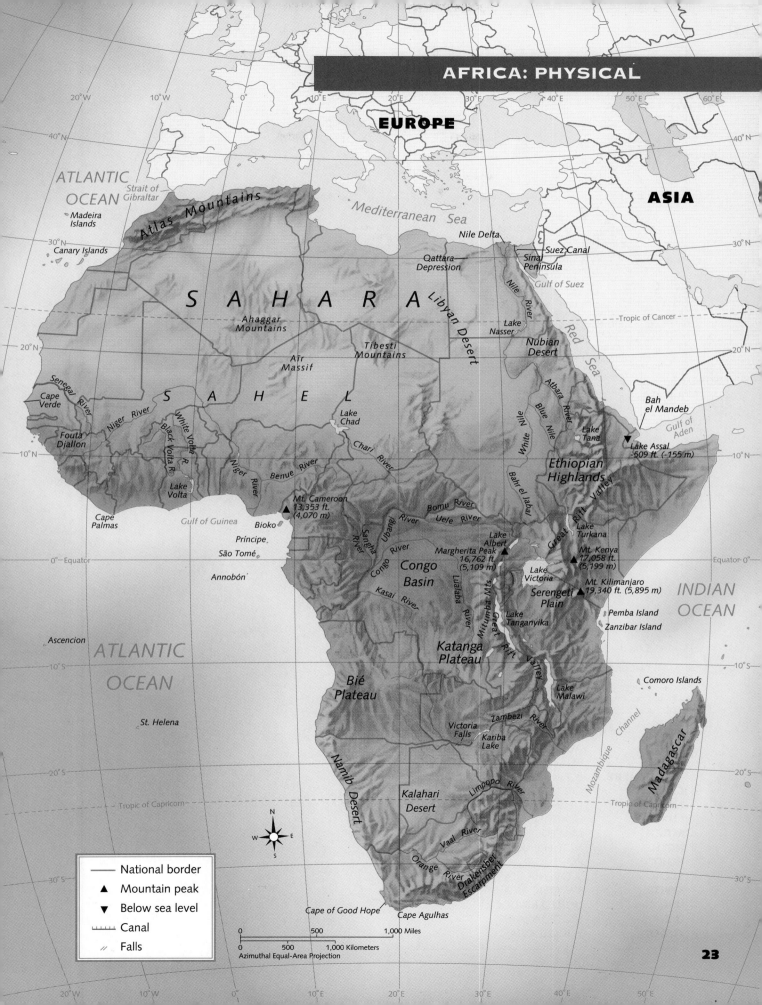

EUROPE

ASIA

ATLANTIC OCEAN

Strait of Gibraltar

Madeira Islands

Canary Islands

Mediterranean Sea

Atlas Mountains

S A H A R A

Ahaggar Mountains

Aïr Massif

Tibesti Mountains

Libyan Desert

Nile Delta

Qattara Depression

Suez Canal

Sinai Peninsula

Gulf of Suez

Tropic of Cancer

Nile River

Lake Nasser

Nubian Desert

Red Sea

S A H E L

Senegal River

Cape Verde

Fouta Djallon

Niger River

White Volta

Black Volta R.

Lake Volta

Niger River

Benue River

Lake Chad

Chari River

Atbara River

Blue Nile

White Nile

Lake Tana

Bahr el Jabal

Ethiopian Highlands

Gulf of Aden

Bab el Mandeb

Lake Assal -509 ft. (-155 m)

Cape Palmas

Gulf of Guinea

Bioko

Príncipe

São Tomé

Annobón

Mt. Cameroon 13,353 ft. (4,070 m)

Bomu River

Uele River

Sangha River

Ubangi River

Congo River

Kasai River

Congo Basin

Luluaba River

Margherita Peak 16,762 ft. (5,109 m)

Lake Albert

Mitumba Mts.

Lake Victoria

Great Rift Valley

Lake Turkana

Mt. Kenya 17,058 ft. (5,199 m)

Mt. Kilimanjaro 19,340 ft. (5,895 m)

Serengeti Plain

Pemba Island

Zanzibar Island

INDIAN OCEAN

Equator

Ascencion

ATLANTIC OCEAN

St. Helena

Bié Plateau

Katanga Plateau

Lake Tanganyika

Great Rift Valley

Lake Malawi

Comoro Islands

Victoria Falls

Zambezi River

Kariba Lake

Namib Desert

Kalahari Desert

Limpopo River

Mozambique Channel

Madagascar

Tropic of Capricorn

Vaal River

Orange River

Drakensberg Escarpment

Cape of Good Hope

Cape Agulhas

N
W   E
S

Legend
— National border
▲ Mountain peak
▼ Below sea level
⊔⊔⊔ Canal
⫽ Falls

0   500   1,000 Miles
0   500   1,000 Kilometers
Azimuthal Equal-Area Projection

23

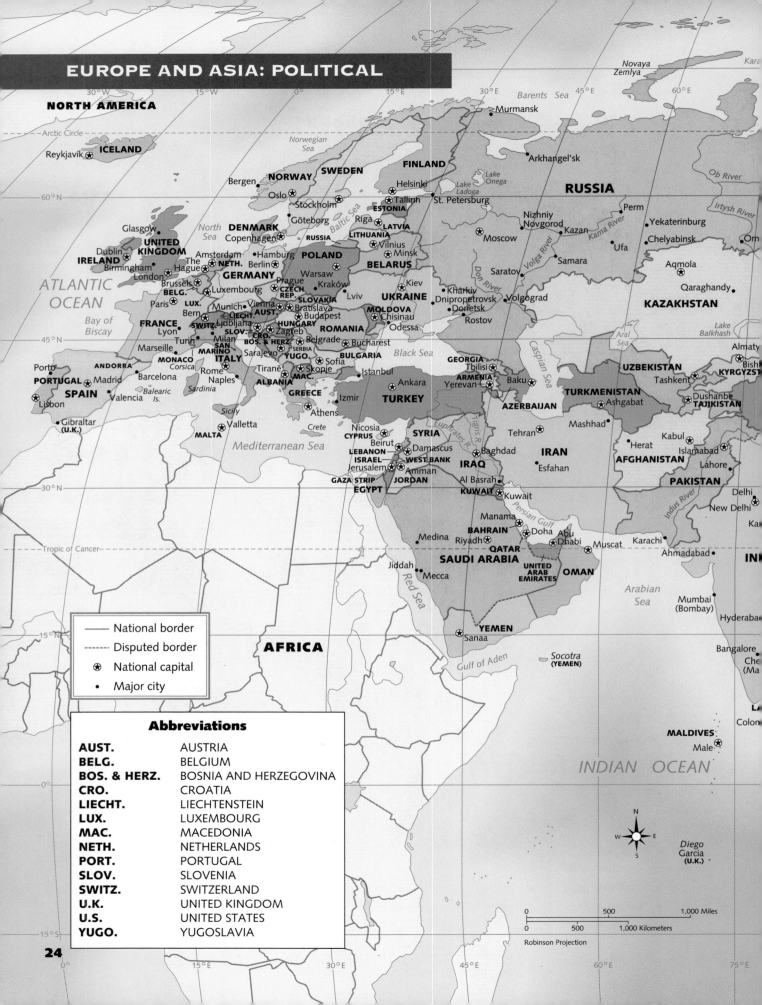

EUROPE AND ASIA: POLITICAL

NORTH AMERICA

Arctic Circle

Reykjavík ⊛ **ICELAND**

Norwegian Sea

60°N

Bergen • **NORWAY** **SWEDEN** **FINLAND**
Oslo ⊛
Göteborg • Stockholm ⊛ Helsinki ⊛

Murmansk •

Barents Sea

Arkhangel'sk • **RUSSIA**

Glasgow • **DENMARK** *North Sea* Copenhagen ⊛ **RUSSIA** **ESTONIA** Tallinn ⊛ St. Petersburg • Perm •

Dublin ⊛ **UNITED KINGDOM** Birmingham • Hamburg • **POLAND** **LATVIA** Riga ⊛ *Lake Ladoga* *Lake Onega* Nizhniy Novgorod • Yekaterinburg •

IRELAND London ⊛ Amsterdam ⊛ Berlin ⊛ Warsaw ⊛ **LITHUANIA** Vilnius ⊛ Minsk ⊛ **BELARUS** Moscow ⊛ Kazan • *Kama River* Chelyabinsk • Om

The Hague • **NETH.** **GERMANY** Prague ⊛ Kraków • Kiev ⊛ *Don River* Saratov • Ufa • Om

ATLANTIC OCEAN Brussels ⊛ **BELG.** Luxembourg ⊛ **CZECH REP.** **SLOVAKIA** Lviv • **UKRAINE** Kharkiv • *Volga River* Samara • Aqmola •

Paris ⊛ **LUX.** Munich • Vienna ⊛ Bratislava ⊛ **MOLDOVA** Dnipropetrovsk • Volgograd • Qaraghandy •

FRANCE Bern ⊛ **LIECHT.** **AUST.** Budapest ⊛ **HUNGARY** Chisinau ⊛ Donetsk • **KAZAKHSTAN**

Bay of Biscay Lyon • **SWITZ.** Ljubljana ⊛ **SLOV.** Zagreb ⊛ **ROMANIA** Odessa • Rostov • *Lake Balkhash*

45°N Turin • Milan • **SAN MARINO** **CRO.** Belgrade ⊛ Bucharest ⊛ *Aral Sea* Almaty •

Marseille • **BOS. & HERZ.** Sarajevo • **SERBIA** **YUGO.** *Black Sea* **GEORGIA** Tbilisi ⊛ *Caspian Sea* **UZBEKISTAN** Bishi

ANDORRA **MONACO** *Corsica* Rome ⊛ **ITALY** Sofia ⊛ **BULGARIA** **ARMENIA** Baku ⊛ Tashkent ⊛ **KYRGYZST**

PORTUGAL Madrid ⊛ Barcelona • *Sardinia* Naples • Tiranë ⊛ Skopje ⊛ **MAC.** Istanbul • Ankara ⊛ Yerevan ⊛ **AZERBAIJAN** **TURKMENISTAN** Dushanbe ⊛ **TAJIKISTAN**

SPAIN Valencia • *Balearic Is.* **ALBANIA** **GREECE** Izmir • **TURKEY** Mashhad • Ashgabat ⊛

Porto • Lisbon ⊛ Gibraltar (U.K.) *Sicily* Valletta ⊛ *Crete* Athens ⊛ Nicosia ⊛ **CYPRUS** Beirut ⊛ **SYRIA** Tehran ⊛ Herat • Kabul ⊛ Islamabad ⊛

30°N **MALTA** *Mediterranean Sea* **LEBANON** Damascus ⊛ Baghdad ⊛ **IRAN** **AFGHANISTAN** Lahore •

ISRAEL **WEST BANK** Amman ⊛ **IRAQ** Esfahan • **PAKISTAN**

Jerusalem ⊛ **GAZA STRIP** **JORDAN** Al Basrah • New Delhi ⊛ Delhi

EGYPT **KUWAIT** Kuwait ⊛ *Indus River* Kar

Manama ⊛ *Persian Gulf* Karachi • Ahmadabad • IN

BAHRAIN Doha ⊛ Abu Dhabi ⊛ Muscat ⊛

Tropic of Cancer Medina • Riyadh ⊛ **QATAR** **UNITED ARAB EMIRATES** **OMAN** *Arabian Sea* Mumbai (Bombay) • Hyderaba

Jiddah • **SAUDI ARABIA** Mecca •

15°N

AFRICA **YEMEN** Sanaa ⊛ Bangalore • Che (Ma

Socotra (YEMEN) *Gulf of Aden* Hyderaba

MALDIVES Male ⊛ Colon

INDIAN OCEAN

LA

Legend

— National border
---- Disputed border
⊛ National capital
• Major city

Abbreviations

AUST.	AUSTRIA
BELG.	BELGIUM
BOS. & HERZ.	BOSNIA AND HERZEGOVINA
CRO.	CROATIA
LIECHT.	LIECHTENSTEIN
LUX.	LUXEMBOURG
MAC.	MACEDONIA
NETH.	NETHERLANDS
PORT.	PORTUGAL
SLOV.	SLOVENIA
SWITZ.	SWITZERLAND
U.K.	UNITED KINGDOM
U.S.	UNITED STATES
YUGO.	YUGOSLAVIA

N
W ⊕ E
S

Diego Garcia (U.K.)

0   500   1,000 Miles

0   500   1,000 Kilometers

Robinson Projection

EUROPE AND ASIA: PHYSICAL

NORTH AMERICA

Barents Sea

Novaya Zemlya

Norwegian Sea

Arctic Circle

Iceland

Faeroe Islands

Kiolen Mountains

Lapland

Kola Peninsula

White Sea

Mt. Narodnaya 6,214 ft. (1,894 m) ▲

Ob River

West Siberia Plain

Galdhøpiggen 8,100 ft. (2,469 m) ▲

Scandinavian Peninsula

Gulf of Bothnia

Lake Onega

60° N

ATLANTIC OCEAN

Highlands

North Sea

Jutland

Baltic Sea

Lake Ladoga

Volga River

Kama River

British Isles

Ireland

Great Britain

Celtic Sea

Rhine R.

NORTHERN EUROPEAN PLAIN

Central Russian Upland

Oka-Don Lowland

Volga Upland

The Steppes

Kazakh Upland

Lake Balkhash

English Channel

Donets Basin

Bay of Biscay

Mt. Blanc 15,771 ft. (4,807 m) ▲

ALPS

Carpathian Mountains

Danube River

Sea of Azov

Crimea

El'brus 18,510 ft. (5,642 m) ▲

Caspian Lowland

Aral Sea

Turan Lowland

Syr Darya

45° N

Massif Central (Plateau)

Dinaric Alps

Balkan Mts.

Black Sea

Caucasus Mts.

Caspian Sea -92 ft -28 m

Kyzyl Kum (Desert)

TIAN S

Iberian Peninsula

Corsica

Adriatic Sea

Balkan Peninsula

Pindus Mts.

Aegean Sea

Dardanelles

Plateau of Anatolia

Mt. Ararat 16,946 ft. (5,165 m) ▲

Kara Kum (Desert)

Amu Darya

Pamirs

Balearic Islands

Sardinia

Tyrrhenian Sea

Ionian Sea

Sicily

Crete

Cyprus

Mesopotamia

Euphrates R.

Syrian Desert

Elburz Mts.

Mt. Damavand 18,934 ft. (5,771 m) ▲

Dasht-e Kavir (Desert)

K2 28,250 ft. (8,611 m) ▲

HIMALA

Strait of Gibraltar

Dead Sea -1,319 ft. (-402 m) ▼

Sinai Peninsula

30° N

Plateau of Iran

Thar Desert

Persian Gulf

Strait of Hormuz

Gulf of Oman

Narmada

Decca

Tropic of Cancer

Red Sea

Arabian Peninsula

Western Ghats

Plateau

AFRICA

Arabian Sea

15° N

Socotra

Gulf of Aden

INDIAN OCEAN

Sri La

0°

	National border
------	Disputed border
▲	Mountain peak
▼	Point below sea level

N
W E
S

15° S

0 500 1,000 Miles

0 500 1,000 Kilometers

Robinson Projection

ARCTIC OCEAN

75° N

Taimyr Peninsula

Laptev
Sea

New Siberian Islands

East Siberian Sea

Wrangel
Island

Chukchi
Sea

North Siberian Lowland

Central
Siberian
Plateau

Kolyma
Lowland

Arctic Circle

Chukchi
Peninsula

165° W

Bering
Strait

S I B E R I A

Lena River

Kolyma R.

60° N

Bering Sea

Central Range

Kamchatka
Peninsula

Arctic Circle

Lake
Baikal

Yablonovyy Range

Amur River

Sea
of
Okhotsk

Sakhalin

Altai Mountains

Greater Khingan Range

Manchurian Plain

45° N

nggar
Basin

Plateau of
Mongolia

Gobi (Desert)

Hokkaido

▼ Turpan Depression
-505 ft.
(-154 m)

Basin

Qilian Shan

North
China

Huang He

Korean
Peninsula

Sea of
Japan

teau
Tibet

Mt. Everest
29,028 ft.
(8,848 m)

▲

▲ Kanchenjunga
28,208 ft.
(8,598 m)

Brahmaputra River

Ganges R.

Sichuan
Basin

Chiang Jiang

Yellow
Sea

Plain

Honshu
▲ Mt. Fuji
12,388 ft.
(3,776 m)

Shikoku

Kyushu

East
China
Sea

30° N

PACIFIC OCEAN

Taiwan

Philippine

Tropic of Cancer

Bay of
Bengal

Gulf
of
Tonkin

Hainan

Sea

Khorat
Plateau

Indochina
Peninsula

South

Luzon

15° N

Andaman
Islands

China

Philippine

Andaman
Sea

Gulf
of
Thailand

Sea

Islands

Nicobar
Islands

Palawan

Malay
Peninsula

Strait of Malacca

Sulu
Sea

Mindanao

Celebes
Sea

Halmahera

0° Equator

Sumatra

Borneo

Moluccas

Greater Sunda

Celebes

▲ Rantekombola
11,335 ft.
(3,455 m)

Ceram

Java Sea

Islands

New Guinea

Java

Bali

Sumbawa

Lombok

Sunda

Sumba

Lesser
Flores
Sunda
Islands

Banda Sea

Timor

Timor
Sea

Arafura Sea

15° S

27

AUSTRALIA

THE WESTERN HEMISPHERE: POLITICAL

ARCTIC OCEAN

Bering Strait

Beaufort Sea

Viscount Melville Sound

Baffin Bay

Greenland **(DENMARK)**

ALASKA **(U.S.)**

Fairbanks

Anchorage

Whitehorse

Juneau

Gulf of Alaska

Bering Sea

Yukon River

Mackenzie River

Liard River

Peace River

Great Bear Lake

Yellowknife

Great Slave Lake

C A N A D A

Athabasca R.

Lake Athabasca

Edmonton

Calgary

Saskatchewan R.

Saskatoon

Regina

Lake Winnipeg

Winnipeg

Thunder Bay

Foxe Basin

Hudson Strait

Hudson Bay

James Bay

Labrador Sea

Arctic Circle

Davis Strait

St. John's

Gulf of St. Lawrence

Vancouver

Seattle

Portland

Boise

Puget Sound

Columbia R.

Snake R.

Great Salt Lake

Salt Lake City

Reno

Las Vegas

San Francisco

Los Angeles

San Diego

Colorado R.

Phoenix

Tucson

Denver

Missouri R.

UNITED STATES

St. Louis

Mississippi R.

Chicago

Memphis

Detroit

Cleveland

Indianapolis

Richmond

Atlanta

Raleigh

Charleston

Savannah

Jacksonville

Tampa

Miami

St. Lawrence River

Great Lakes

Ottawa

Toronto

Albany

Montreal

Québec

St. John

Halifax

Boston

New York City

Philadelphia

Washington, D.C.

Norfolk

ATLANTIC OCEAN

Hermosillo

Chihuahua

El Paso

Dallas

Houston

San Antonio

New Orleans

Rio Grande

Durango

MEXICO

Monterrey

Gulf of Mexico

BAHAMAS

Nassau

Tropic of Cancer

León

Tampico

Guadalajara

Mexico City

Puebla

Veracruz

Acapulco

GUATEMALA

Guatemala

BELIZE

Belmopan

HONDURAS

Tegucigalpa

San Salvador

EL SALVADOR

Managua

NICARAGUA

COSTA RICA

San José

Panama City

PANAMA

Havana

CUBA

JAMAICA

Kingston

HAITI

Port-au-Prince

Santo Domingo

PUERTO RICO (U.S.)

DOMINICAN REPUBLIC

Caribbean Sea

HAWAII **(U.S.)**

Honolulu

PACIFIC OCEAN

Medellín

Cali

Bogotá

COLOMBIA

Quito

Guayaquil

ECUADOR

Iquitos

Maracaibo

Caracas

VENEZUELA

GUYANA

SURINAME

Georgetown

Paramaribo

Cayenne

FRENCH GUIANA (FRANCE)

Galápagos Islands **(ECUADOR)**

Equator

Rio Negro

Manaus

Amazon R.

Belém

Fortaleza

Recife

Tapajós River

Xingu R.

Tocantins R.

FRENCH POLYNESIA **(FRANCE)**

Papeete

Trujillo

PERU

Lima

Cuzco

Lake Titicaca

La Paz

Arequipa

BOLIVIA

Sucre

BRAZIL

Brasília

Goiânia

São Francisco R.

Salvador

Belo Horizonte

Rio de Janeiro

Campo Grande

São Paulo

Curitiba

Tropic of Capricorn

Antofagasta

Salta

San Miguel de Tucumán

PARAGUAY

Asunción

Paraguay R.

CHILE

Córdoba

Valparaíso

Santiago

Concepción

Valdivia

Rosario

Buenos Aires

La Plata

Mar del Plata

Bahía Blanca

Pôrto Alegre

URUGUAY

Montevideo

Rio de la Plata

ARGENTINA

Falkland Islands **(U.K.)**

South Georgia **(U.K.)**

Punta Arenas

0 1,000 2,000 Miles

0 1,000 2,000 Kilometers

Miller Cylindrical Projection

— National border

⊛ National capital

• City

N

W E

S

150° W   120° W   90° W   60° W   30°

60° N

30° N

0°

30° S

THE WESTERN HEMISPHERE: PHYSICAL

ARCTIC OCEAN

North Magnetic Pole +

Queen Elizabeth Islands

Ellesmere Island

Melville island

Devon Island

Greenland

Beaufort Sea

Banks Island

Viscount Melville Sound

Baffin Bay

Point Barrow

Victoria Island

Brooks Range

Mt. McKinley 20,320 ft. (6,194 m)

Yukon River

Great Bear Lake

Baffin Island

Foxe Basin

Davis Strait

Arctic Circle

60° N

Yukon Plateau

Mackenzie River

Liard River

Great Slave Lake

Mackenzie Mts.

Hudson Strait

Alaska Range

Mt. Logan 19,524 ft. (5,951 m)

Coast Mountains

Peace River

Athabasca River

Lake Athabasca

CANADIAN

Hudson Bay

Labrador

Cape Farewell

Gulf of Alaska

Kodiak Island

Alaska Peninsula

Aleutian Islands

Queen Charlotte Islands

Vancouver Island

Puget Sound

ROCKY

Saskatchewan River

Lake Winnipeg

James Bay

SHIELD

Labrador Sea

Newfoundland

Cascade Range

Coast Ranges

MOUNTAINS

GREAT

Missouri R.

Black Hills

Platte R.

PLAINS

Mississippi River

Great Lakes

St. Lawrence R.

Gulf of St. Lawrence

Nova Scotia

Bay of Fundy

Cape Cod

Long Island

Snake R.

Great Salt Lake

GREAT BASIN

Colorado R.

INTERIOR PLAINS

Arkansas

Ohio R.

Ozark Plateau

APPALACHIAN MTS.

Mt. Whitney 14,495 ft. (4,418 m)

Death Valley (lowest point in N.A.) -282 ft. (-86 m)

Sonora Desert

Sierra Madre Occidental

Rio Grande

Mississippi River

COASTAL PLAIN

Cape Hatteras

ATLANTIC OCEAN

30° N

Baja California

Gulf of California

Sierra Madre Oriental

Gulf of Mexico

Bahamas

Hawaiian Islands

Tropic of Cancer

PACIFIC OCEAN

Citlaltepetl 18,701 ft. (5,700 m)

Yucatán Peninsula

Hispaniola

Puerto Rico

Lesser Antilles

Caribbean Sea

Lake Nicaragua

Lake Maracaibo

Llanos

Orinoco R.

Guiana Highlands

Line Islands

Equator

Galápagos Islands

Isthmus of Panama

Chimborazo 20,561 ft. (6,267 m)

AMAZON BASIN

Rio Negro

Amazon R.

Cape São Roque

Marquesas Islands

Huascarán 22,205 ft. (6,768 m)

ANDES

Tapajós River

Xingu River

Tocantins

São Francisco River

Brazilian Highlands

Mato Grosso Plateau

Cook Islands

Society Islands

Tuamotu Archipelago

Lake Titicaca

Tropic of Capricorn

Altiplano

Atacama Desert

Paraguay R.

Paraná

MOUNTAINS

Gran Chaco

Iguazú Falls

Uruguay R.

30° S

0   1,000   2,000 Miles

0   1,000   2,000 Kilometers

Miller Cylindrical Projection

Mt. Aconcagua 22,831 ft. (6,959 m)

Pampa

Rio de la Plata

▲ Mountain peak

▼ Point below sea level

— National border

≈ Waterfall

N
W   E
S

Valdés Peninsula (lowest point in S.A.) -131 ft. (-40 m)

Falkland Islands

29

Strait of Magellan

Tierra del Fuego

Cape Horn

South Georgia

150° W   120° W   90° W   60° W   30° W

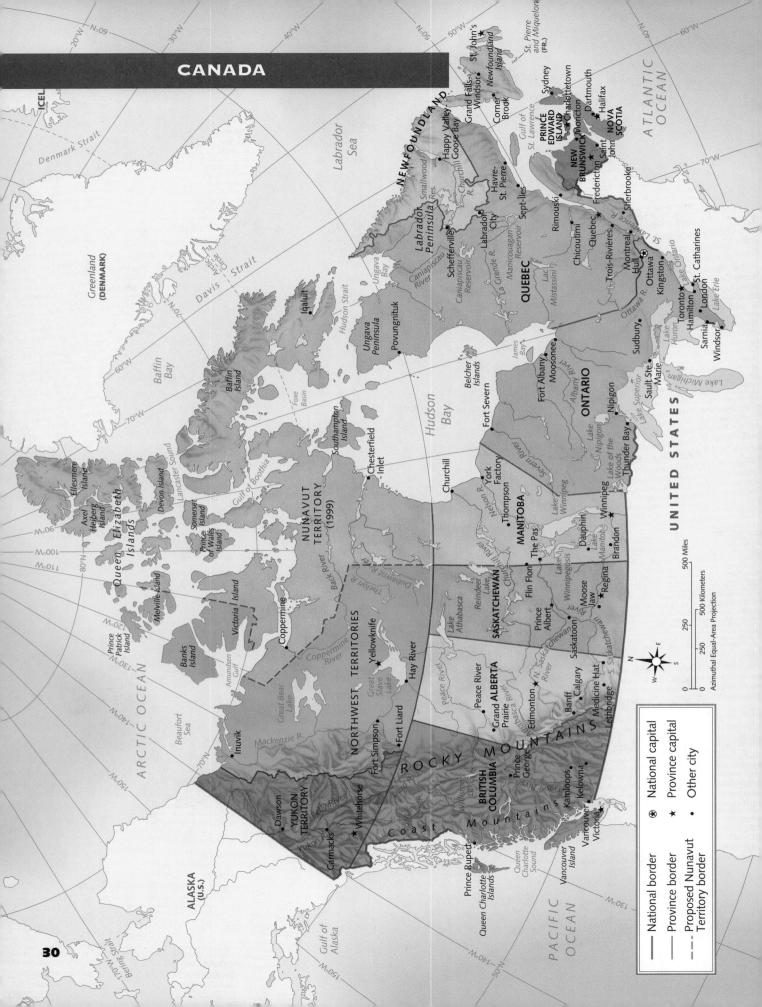

CANADA

ICELAND

Greenland (DENMARK)

Denmark Strait

Labrador Sea

Arctic Circle

Davis Strait

Baffin Bay

Baffin Island

Foxe Basin

ATLANTIC OCEAN

St. John's

St. Pierre and Miquelon (FR.)

Newfoundland Island

NEWFOUNDLAND

Grand Falls · Windsor

Corner Brook

Gulf of St. Lawrence

Sydney

Charlottetown

PRINCE EDWARD ISLAND

Moncton

Dartmouth

Halifax

NOVA SCOTIA

Fredericton · Saint John

NEW BRUNSWICK

Sherbrooke

Happy Valley Goose Bay

Churchill R.

Havre-St. Pierre

Sept-Îles

Rimouski

Chicoutimi

Québec

Trois-Rivières

Montreal

Hull

St. Lawrence R.

Labrador Peninsula

Schefferville

Labrador City

Caniapiscau Reservoir

Caniapiscau River

Smallwood Res.

Manicouagan Reservoir

La Grande R.

Lac Mistassini

QUEBEC

Lac St.-Jean

Ottawa R.

Ottawa

Kingston

Lake Ontario

Toronto

Hamilton

St. Catharines

London

Sarnia

Windsor

Lake Erie

Ungava Bay

Ungava Peninsula

Povungnituk

Belcher Islands

James Bay

Fort Albany

Moosonee

ONTARIO

Albany River

Lake Superior

Sudbury

Sault Ste. Marie

Lake Huron

Lake Michigan

Hudson Strait

Hudson Bay

Fort Severn

York Factory

Churchill

Nelson River

Thompson

MANITOBA

Winnipeg

Lake Winnipeg

Dauphin

Brandon

Lake Manitoba

Nipigon

Lake Nipigon

Thunder Bay

Lake of the Woods

Fort Severn

Iqaluit

Southampton Island

Chesterfield Inlet

NUNAVUT TERRITORY (1999)

Back River

Thelon R.

Dubawnt River

Reindeer Lake

Lake Athabasca

SASKATCHEWAN

Prince Albert

Flin Flon

The Pas

Lake Winnipegosis

Saskatoon

Moose Jaw

Regina

S. Saskatchewan River

N. Saskatchewan River

Churchill R.

Ellesmere Island

Axel Heiberg Island

Queen Elizabeth Islands

Devon Island

Prince of Wales Island

Somerset Island

Melville Island

Prince Patrick Island

Banks Island

Victoria Island

Lancaster Sound

Gulf of Boothia

Coppermine

Coppermine River

Amundsen Gulf

Beaufort Sea

NORTHWEST TERRITORIES

Great Bear Lake

Great Slave Lake

Yellowknife

Hay River

Fort Liard

Fort Simpson

Mackenzie R.

Inuvik

ARCTIC OCEAN

UNITED STATES

ALBERTA

Peace River

Peace River

Grand Prairie

Edmonton

Calgary

Banff

Red Deer River

Medicine Hat

Lethbridge

Athabasca River

ROCKY MOUNTAINS

BRITISH COLUMBIA

Prince George

Kamloops

Kelowna

Vancouver

Victoria

Vancouver Island

Fraser River

Coast Mountains

Prince Rupert

Queen Charlotte Islands

Queen Charlotte Sound

PACIFIC OCEAN

YUKON TERRITORY

Dawson

Whitehorse

Carmacks

Yukon R.

Pelly River

Liard R.

ALASKA (U.S.)

Gulf of Alaska

Bering Strait

500 Miles

500 Kilometers

250

250

Azimuthal Equal-Area Projection

N

S

E

W

National border	⊛ National capital
Province border	★ Province capital
Proposed Nunavut Territory border	• Other city

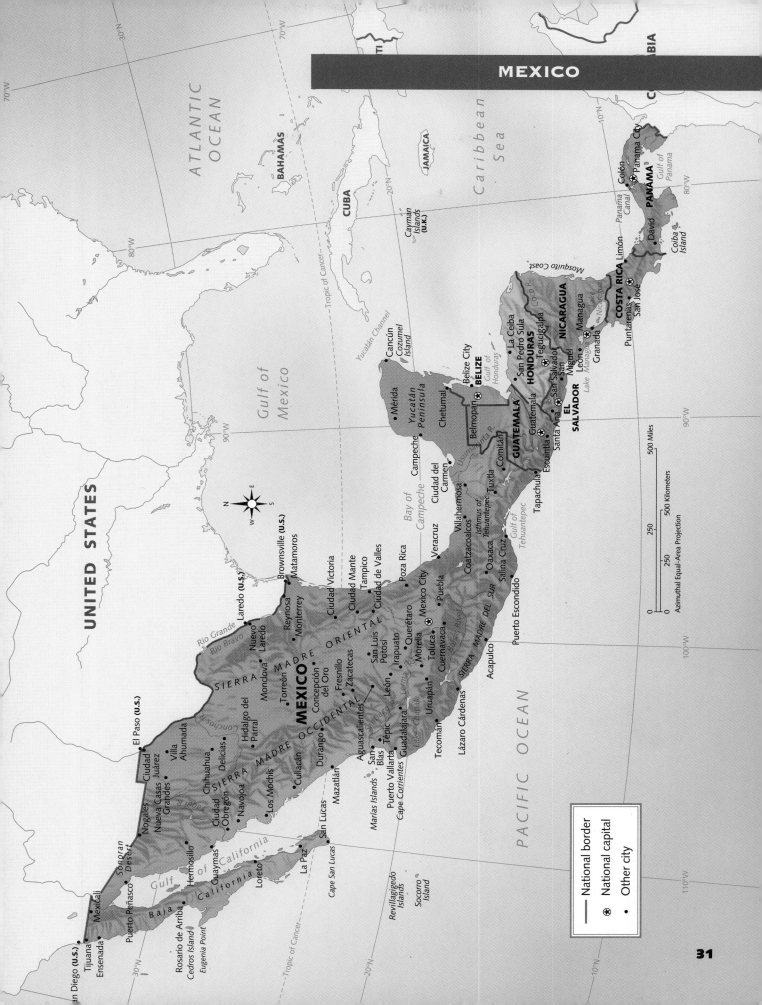

ATLANTIC
OCEAN

BAHAMAS

CUBA

JAMAICA

Cayman
Islands
(U.K.)

Caribbean
Sea

Tropic of Cancer

Yucatán Channel

Gulf of
Mexico

Cancún
Cozumel
Island

Mérida
Yucatán
Peninsula

Campeche

Bay of
Campeche

Ciudad del
Carmen

Chetumal

Belize City
BELIZE
Belmopan

Mosquito Coast

La Ceiba
San Pedro Sula
HONDURAS
Tegucigalpa

NICARAGUA

Managua
León
Granada

Lake
Managua

Lake
Nicaragua

Limón
COSTA RICA
San José

Puntarenas

Colón
Panama
Canal
PANAMA
David

Gulf of
Panama

Coiba
Island

Panama City

UNITED STATES

N
W E
S

Brownsville (U.S.)
Matamoros

Reynosa
Monterrey
Nuevo
Laredo
Laredo (U.S.)

Rio Grande
Rio Bravo

El Paso (U.S.)
Ciudad
Juárez

Nueva Casas
Grandes

Villa
Ahumada

Chihuahua
Delicias
Hidalgo del
Parral

SIERRA MADRE OCCIDENTAL

Monclova
Torreón
Concepción
del Oro
Fresnillo
Zacatecas

Ciudad Victoria
Ciudad Mante
Tampico
Ciudad de Valles
Poza Rica
Veracruz
Villahermosa
Coatzacoalcos

Isthmus of
Tehuantepec

Salina Cruz

Gulf of
Tehuantepec

MEXICO
SIERRA MADRE ORIENTAL

San Luis
Potosí
Irapuato
León
Aguascalientes
Tepic

Querétaro
Mexico City
Toluca
Cuernavaca
Morelia
Uruapán

Puebla

Oaxaca

SIERRA MADRE DEL SUR

Puerto Escondido

PACIFIC OCEAN

Durango
Culiacán

San
Blas
Guadalajara
Tecomán
Lázaro Cárdenas
Acapulco

Navojoa
Los Mochis
Ciudad
Obregón

Mazatlán
Puerto Vallarta
Cape Corrientes

Marías Islands

Nogales

Sonoran
Desert

Hermosillo
Guaymas

Gulf of California

Puerto Peñasco

Mexicali

San Diego (U.S.)
Tijuana
Ensenada

Rosario de Arriba
Cedros Island
Eugenia Point

Baja California

La Paz
Loreto

San Lucas
Cape San Lucas

Revillagigedo
Islands
Socorro
Island

Tropic of Cancer

GUATEMALA
Guatemala
Comitán
Tuxtla
Tapachula
Escuintla
Santa Ana
Tapachula

EL SALVADOR
San Salvador
San
Miguel

Usumacinta R.

Grijalva R.

Coco R.

| | 500 Miles |
| 0 250 500 Kilometers |

Azimuthal Equal-Area Projection

Legend:
— National border
⊛ National capital
• Other city

CARIBBEAN ISLANDS

National border —
National capital ⊛
Other city •

ATLANTIC OCEAN

BAHAMAS

Grand Bahama
Great Abaco
Freeport
Eleuthera
Nassau ⊛
New Providence
Cat Island
Great Exuma
Andros I.
San Salvador
Long Island
Acklins Island
Crooked Island
Great Inagua
Mayaguana
TURKS AND CAICOS IS. (U.K.)

UNITED STATES
Straits of Florida
Gulf of Mexico
Havana ⊛
Matanzas
Pinar del Río
Cape San Antonio
Nueva Gerona
Isla de la Juventud
Santa Clara
Cienfuegos
CUBA
Camagüey
Victoria de las Tunas
Manzanillo
Holguín
Bayamo
Santiago de Cuba
Guantánamo
CAYMAN IS. (U.K.)
George Town

Windward Passage
Cap-Haïtien
Gonaïves
HAITI
Port-au-Prince
Hispaniola
Santiago
Cape Falso

JAMAICA
Montego Bay
Kingston ⊛

Greater Antilles

Santo Domingo
San Pedro de Macorís
DOMINICAN REPUBLIC
Cape Beata

Caribbean Sea

Mona Passage
PUERTO RICO (U.S.)
San Juan
Mayagüez
Ponce
St. Croix
Virgin Is. (U.K.)
Virgin Is. (U.S.)

ANGUILLA (U.K.)
ST. MARTIN (FRANCE AND NETHE
ST. BARTHÉLEMY (FRANCE)
NETH. ANTILLES (NETH.)
ST. KITTS AND NEVIS
Basseterre
Barbuda
ANTIGUA AND BARBUDA
St. John's
Antigua
MONTSERRAT (U.K.)
GUADELOUPE (FRANCE)
Pointe-à-Pitre
DOMINICA
Roseau
MARTINIQUE (FR.)
Fort-de-France
Castries
ST. LUCIA
Kingstown
ST. VINCENT AND THE GRENADINES
BARBADOS
Bridgetown
St. George's
GRENADA
Tobago
TRINIDAD AND TOBAGO
Port-of-Spain
Trinidad

Leeward Islands
Windward Islands
Lesser Antilles
Margarita I. (VENEZUELA)
Tortuga I. (VENEZUELA)

NETHERLANDS ANTILLES (NETHERLANDS)
Bonaire
Curaçao
Willemstad
ARUBA (NETHERLANDS)
Oranjestad

VENEZUELA
COLOMBIA

HONDURAS
NICARAGUA
COSTA RICA

W E S T   I N D I E S

N
E
S
W

200 Miles
100   200 Kilometers
0
0   100   200
Lambert Conformal Conic Projection

55°W
60°W
65°W
70°W
75°W
80°W
85°W

25°N
20°N
15°N
10°N

Tropic of Cancer

Caribbean Sea

ARUBA (NETH.)   NETH. ANTILLES (NETH.)

80°W

Barranquilla
Cartagena
COSTA RICA
PANAMA
Medellín
Manizales
Pereira
Ibagué
Cali
COLOMBIA
Cúcuta
San Cristóbal
Bucaramanga
Bogotá

Maracaibo
Lake Maracaibo
Valencia   Caracas   Cumaná
Maracay   Maturín
Barquisimeto
Ciudad Guayana
Ciudad Bolívar
VENEZUELA
GUYANA
Orinoco River
Llanos
Guiana   Highlands
Orinoco R.

TRINIDAD AND TOBAGO

60°W

Georgetown
Paramaribo
SURINAME
FRENCH GUIANA (FR.)
Cayenne

50°W   40°W

10°N

ATLANTIC
OCEAN

Quito
ECUADOR
Guayaquil   Ambato
Cuenca
Iquitos
Aguja Point
Chiclayo
Trujillo
PERU
Callao
Lima
Huancayo
Cuzco

0° Equator

Marañón River
Putumayo R.
Río Negro
Río Negro
A M A Z O N
S e l v a s
B A S I N
La Montaña
Ucayali River
Purus R.
Juruá River
Madeira River
Amazon River
Manaus
Santarém
Tapajós River
Xingu
River
Araguaia River
Tocantins River

Marajó Island
Belém
São Luís

0° Equator

Fortaleza
Teresina
Natal
João Pessoa
Recife
Maceió

BRAZIL

10°S

Arequipa
Arica
Iquique
Antofagasta

Lake Titicaca
BOLIVIA
La Paz
Cochabamba
Sucre
Tarija
Altiplano
Atacama Desert
ANDES   MOUNTAINS
Beni R.
Mamoré River
Guaporé River
Santa Cruz
Mato Grosso
Plateau
Gran Chaco
Pilcomayo R.
Paraguay River
Campo Grande
PARAGUAY
Asunción
Paraná River
Itaipú Reservoir

Brazilian
Highlands
Brasília
Goiânia
Ribeirão Prêto
Campos
Londrina
Sorocaba
São Paulo
Campinas
Curitiba
Belo Horizonte
Vitória
Juiz de Fora
Volta Redonda
Niterói
Rio de Janeiro
Santos
Salvador
Aracaju

10°S

20°S

Tropic of Capricorn

San Ambrosio Island (CHILE)
San Félix Island (CHILE)
Juan Fernández Islands (CHILE)

Salta
San Miguel de Tucumán
Santiago del Estero
Córdoba
San Juan
Mendoza
Viña del Mar
Valparaíso
Santiago
CHILE
Resistencia
Santa Fe
Rosario
Paraná River
Salado R.
Pampas
Uruguay R.
Rivera
Salto
Paysandú
Pelotas
Pôrto Alegre
URUGUAY
Buenos Aires
Avellaneda
La Plata
Montevideo
Río de la Plata

20°S

Tropic of Capricorn

30°S

PACIFIC
OCEAN

Talcahuano
Concepción
Temuco
ARGENTINA
Colorado R.
Mar del Plata
Bahía Blanca

30°S

ATLANTIC
OCEAN

Puerto Montt
Chiloé Island
Chonos Archipelago
Taitao Peninsula

San Matías Gulf
Valdés Peninsula
Patagonia
Gulf of San Jorge
Cape Tres Puntas

40°S

	National border
⊛	National capital
•	Other city

N
W   E
S

300   600 Miles
0   300   600 Kilometers
Bipolar Oblique Conic Projection

Bahía Grande
Punta Arenas
Strait of Magellan
Tierra del Fuego
Ushuaia
Cape Horn

Stanley
Falkland Islands (U.K.)
(Islas Malvinas)

South Georgia (U.K.)

50°S

90°W   80°W   70°W   60°W   50°W   40°W   30°W   20°W

THE PACIFIC RIM: POLITICAL AND PHYSICAL

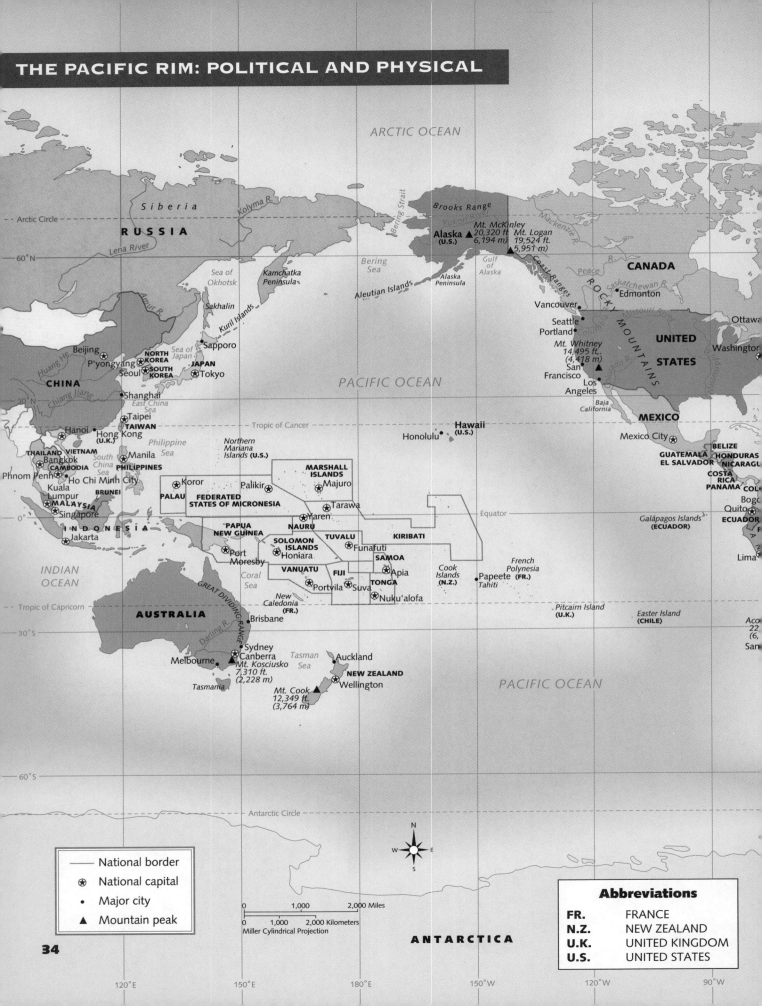

ARCTIC OCEAN

Siberia

Kolyma R.

Brooks Range

Alaska ▲ Mt. McKinley
(U.S.) 20,320 ft
6,194 m)   Mt. Logan
            19,524 ft.
            5,951 m)

R U S S I A

Lena River

Arctic Circle

60°N

*Sea of
Okhotsk*

*Kamchatka
Peninsula*

*Bering
Sea*

Bering Strait

Yukon River

*Gulf
of
Alaska*

*Alaska
Peninsula*

Aleutian Islands

Coast Ranges

Mackenzie R.

CANADA

Peace R.

Saskatchewan R.

Edmonton

Amur R.

Sakhalin

Kuril Islands

*Sea of
Japan*

Sapporo

Vancouver

Seattle
Portland

Columbia R.

Missouri River

R O C K Y   M O U N T A I N S

UNITED

STATES

Ottawa

Beijing
P'yongyang
Seoul

NORTH
KOREA
SOUTH
KOREA

JAPAN
Tokyo

Mt. Whitney
14,495 ft.
(4,418 m)
San
Francisco

Washington

Huang He

CHINA

Shanghai

*East China
Sea*

PACIFIC OCEAN

Los
Angeles

Rio Grande

*Baja
California*

MEXICO

Chiang Jiang

Taipei

TAIWAN

Tropic of Cancer

Hawaii
(U.S.)

Mexico City

BELIZE

Hanoi
THAILAND VIETNAM
Bangkok
CAMBODIA
Phnom Penh
Kuala
Lumpur
MALAYSIA
BRUNEI

Hong Kong
(U.K.)

*Philippine
Sea*

Manila

PHILIPPINES

*South
China
Sea*

Ho Chi Minh City

Honolulu

Northern
Mariana
Islands (U.S.)

MARSHALL
ISLANDS

Majuro

GUATEMALA
EL SALVADOR

HONDURAS
NICARAGU

COSTA
RICA
PANAMA

Koror
PALAU

Palikir
FEDERATED
STATES OF
MICRONESIA

Tarawa

Singapore

I N D O N E S I A

Jakarta

PAPUA
NEW GUINEA

Yaren
NAURU

SOLOMON
ISLANDS
Honiara

TUVALU
Funafuti

KIRIBATI

Equator

Galápagos Islands
(ECUADOR)

Bogo
Quito
ECUADOR

COL

INDIAN
OCEAN

Port
Moresby

VANUATU

Portvila

*Coral
Sea*

FIJI

Suva

SAMOA
Apia

TONGA
Nuku'alofa

Cook
Islands
(N.Z.)

French
Polynesia
(FR.)
Papeete
Tahiti

Lima

Tropic of Capricorn

AUSTRALIA

GREAT DIVIDING RANGE

*New
Caledonia
(FR.)*

Pitcairn Island
(U.K.)

Easter Island
(CHILE)

Aco
22
(6,
San

30°S

Darling R.

Brisbane

Sydney
Melbourne   Canberra
        ▲ Mt. Kosciusko
          7,310 ft.
          (2,228 m)

*Tasman
Sea*

Auckland

PACIFIC OCEAN

Tasmania

NEW ZEALAND
Wellington

Mt. Cook
12,349 ft.
(3,764 m)

60°S

Antarctic Circle

N
W   E
S

Legend:
— National border
⊛ National capital
• Major city
▲ Mountain peak

0   1,000   2,000 Miles
0   1,000 2,000 Kilometers
Miller Cylindrical Projection

A N T A R C T I C A

Abbreviations	
FR.	FRANCE
N.Z.	NEW ZEALAND
U.K.	UNITED KINGDOM
U.S.	UNITED STATES

120°E   150°E   180°   150°W   120°W   90°W

MAJOR RIVERS OF THE WORLD

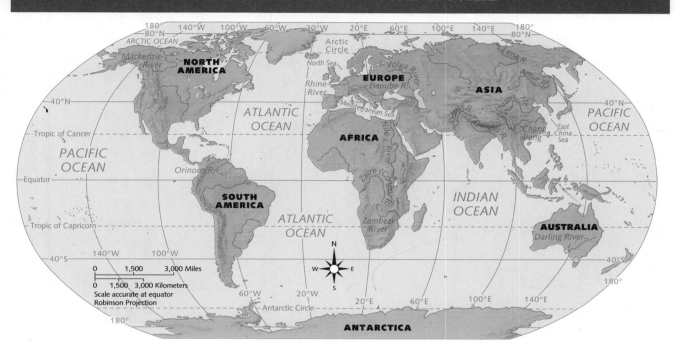

THE WORLD'S MAJOR RIVERS

RIVER	LENGTH		CONTINENT
	in miles	in kilometers	
Nile	4,187	6,738	Africa
Amazon	4,000	6,437	South America
Chang Jiang	3,434	5,526	Asia
Mississippi	2,348	3,779	North America
Volga	2,293	3,690	Europe
Darling	1,702	2,739	Australia
Ganges	1,557	2,506	Asia
Rhine	820	1,320	Europe

MOUNTAINS OF THE WORLD

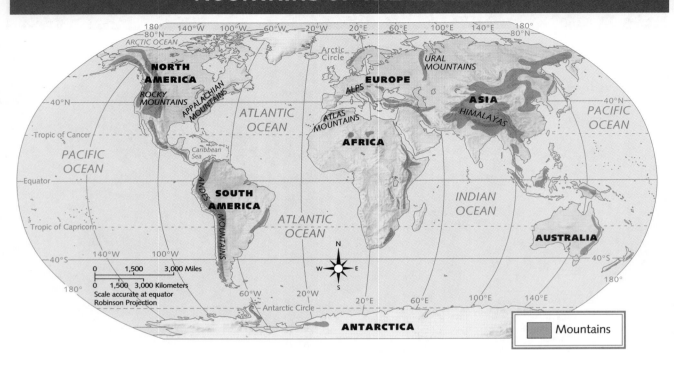

HIGHEST MOUNTAIN ON EACH CONTINENT

MAJOR PLAINS OF THE WORLD

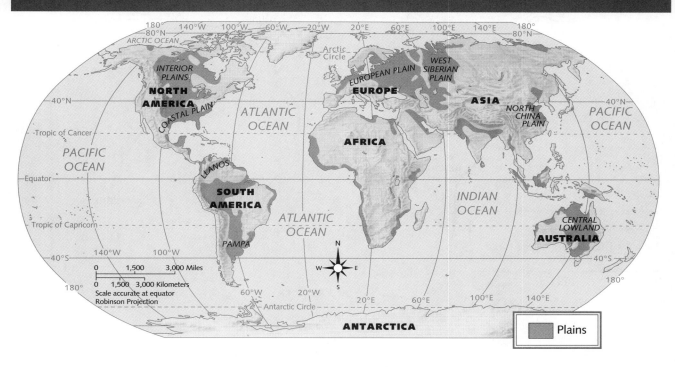

MAJOR DESERTS OF THE WORLD

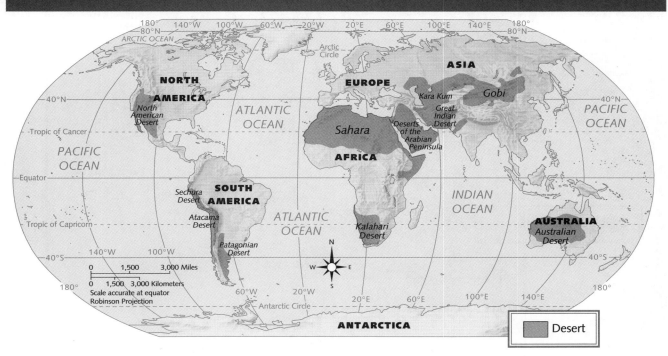

MIGRATION OF EARLY PEOPLE

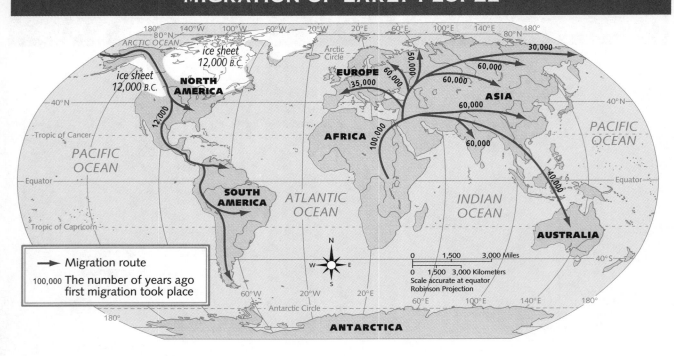

EARLY FARMING AREAS

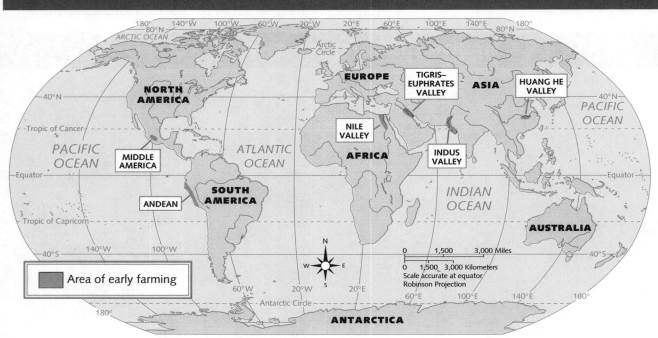

MAJOR CITIES OF THE 1400s

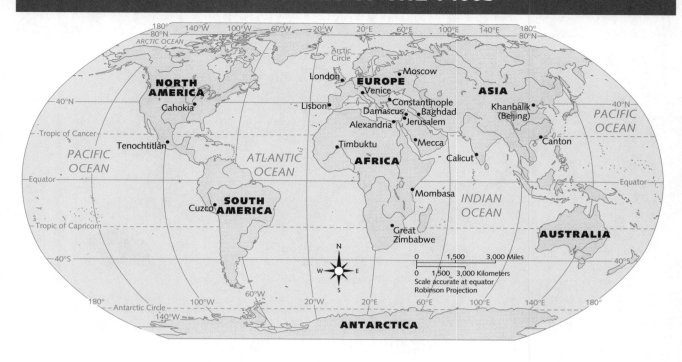

VOYAGES OF EXPLORATION

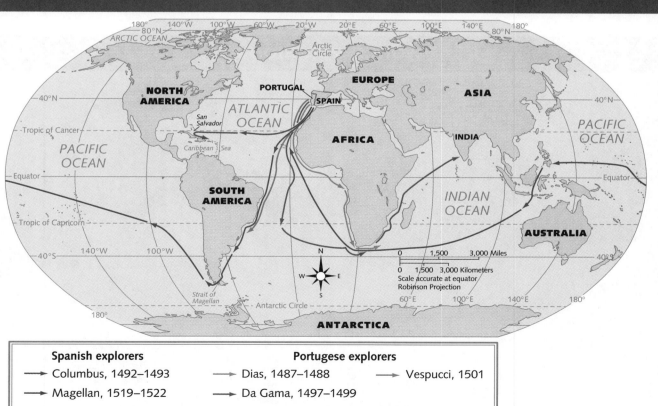

Spanish explorers	Portugese explorers	
→ Columbus, 1492–1493	→ Dias, 1487–1488	→ Vespucci, 1501
→ Magellan, 1519–1522	→ Da Gama, 1497–1499	

WORLD LANGUAGES

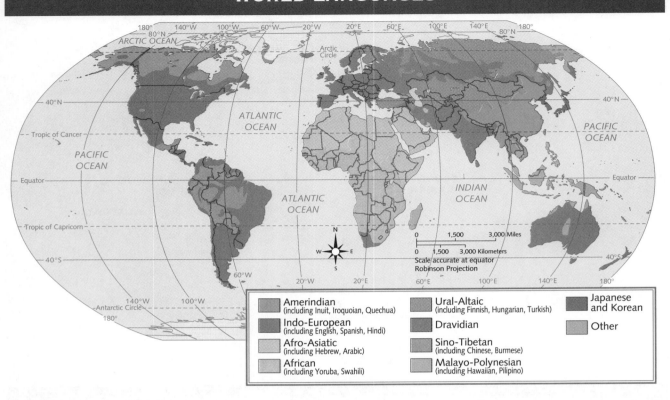

■	**Amerindian** (including Inuit, Iroquoian, Quechua)	■	**Ural-Altaic** (including Finnish, Hungarian, Turkish)	■	**Japanese and Korean**
■	**Indo-European** (including English, Spanish, Hindi)	■	**Dravidian**	■	**Other**
■	**Afro-Asiatic** (including Hebrew, Arabic)	■	**Sino-Tibetan** (including Chinese, Burmese)		
■	**African** (including Yoruba, Swahili)	■	**Malayo-Polynesian** (including Hawaiian, Pilipino)		

WORLD RELIGIONS

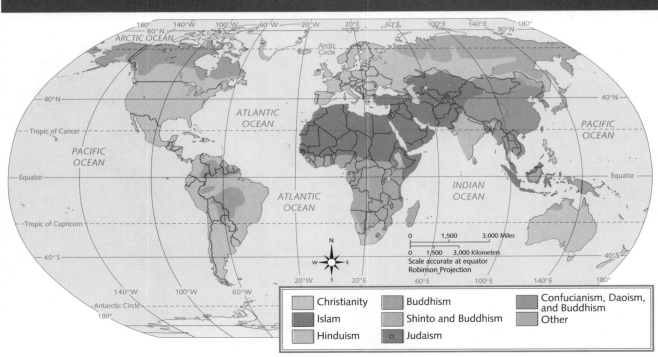

■	Christianity	■	Buddhism	■	Confucianism, Daoism, and Buddhism
■	Islam	■	Shinto and Buddhism	■	Other
■	Hinduism	✡	Judaism		

TIME ZONES OF THE WORLD

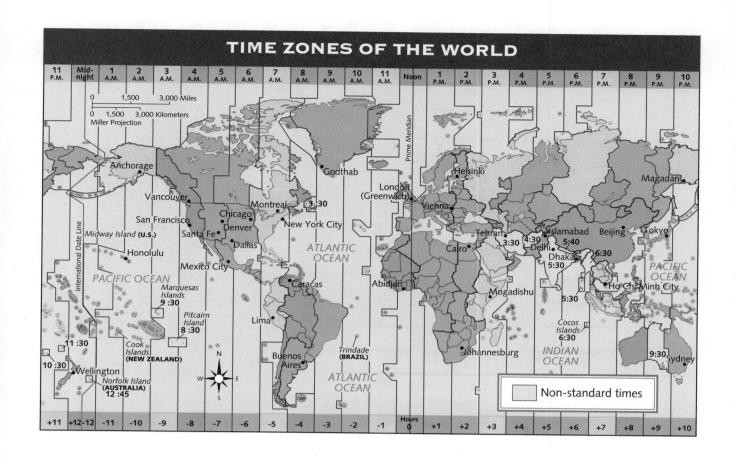

CLOCKS AROUND THE WORLD

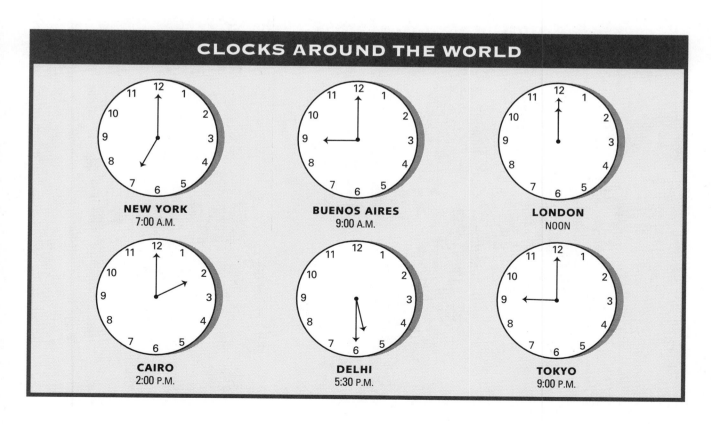

NEW YORK
7:00 A.M.

BUENOS AIRES
9:00 A.M.

LONDON
NOON

CAIRO
2:00 P.M.

DELHI
5:30 P.M.

TOKYO
9:00 P.M.

POLITICAL MAP OF THE WORLD

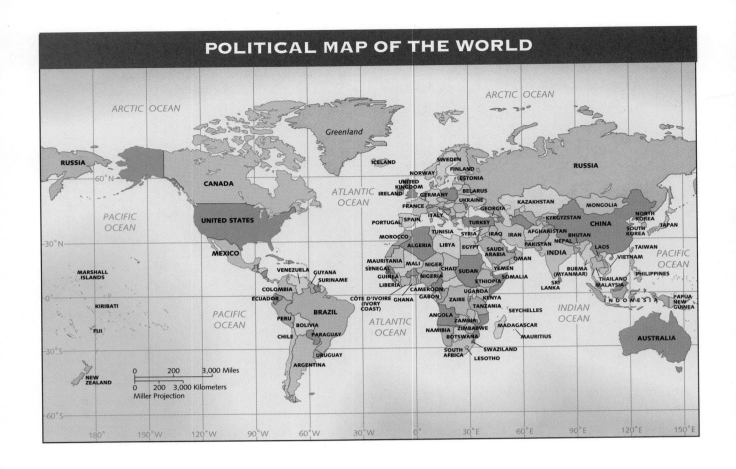

WORLD POPULATION CARTOGRAM

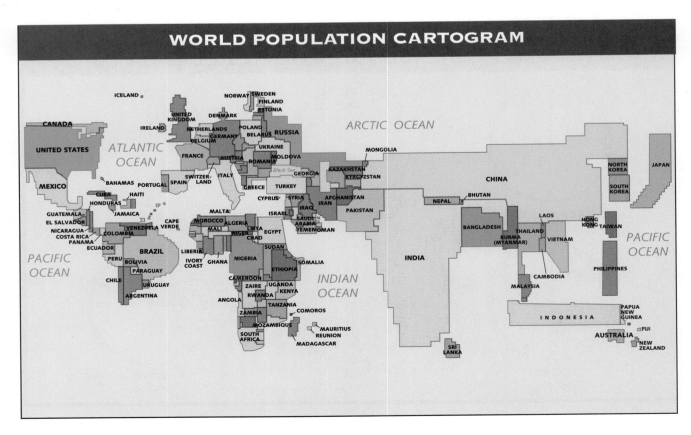

CARTOGRAM: GROSS DOMESTIC PRODUCT

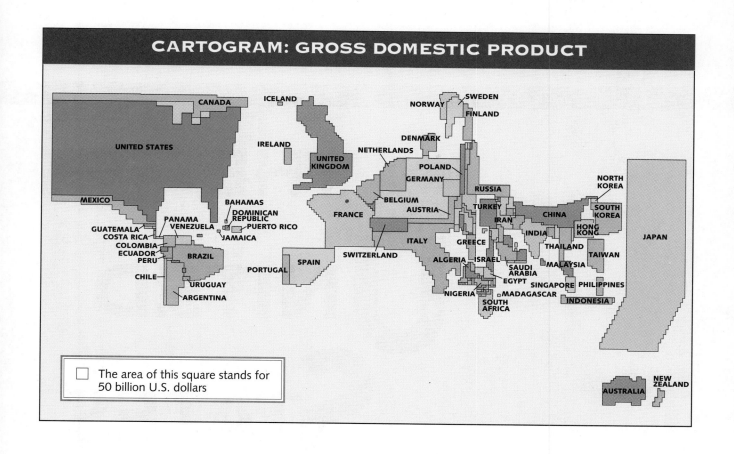

The area of this square stands for 50 billion U.S. dollars

GDP FOR SELECTED COUNTRIES

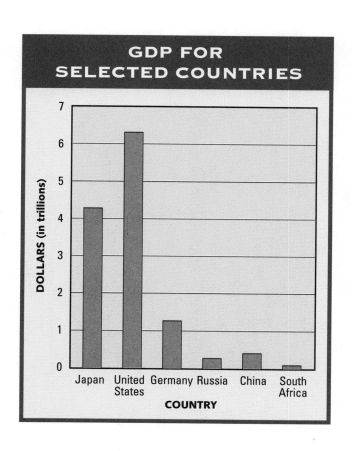

DOLLARS (in trillions)

COUNTRY

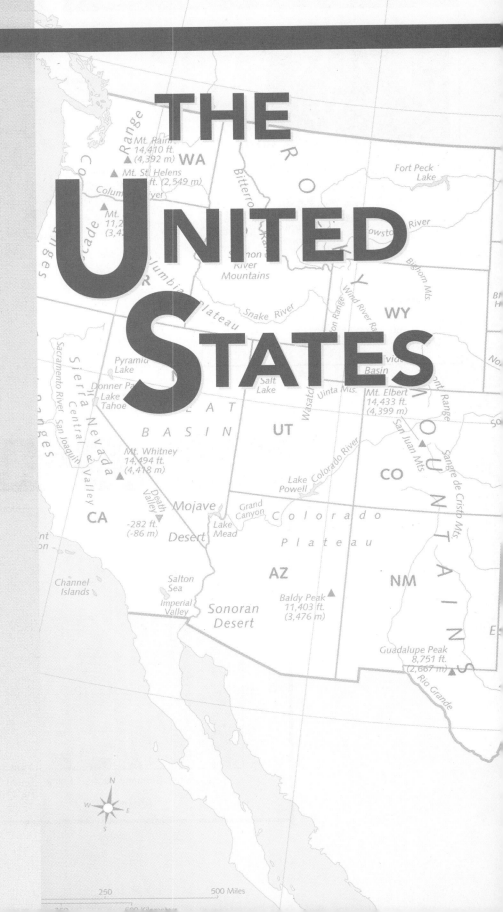

THE UNITED STATES

120°W

110°W

Range

Mt. Rain.
14,410 ft.
▲ (4,392 m)

WA

▲ Mt. St. Helens
ft. (2,549 m)

Columbia River

Mt.
11,2
(3,4

Cascade

ges

Columbia Plateau

Bitterro

Salmon River
Mountains

Snake River

Y

on Range

Wind River Ra

WY

owsto

River

Bighorn Mts.

Fort Peck
Lake

BI
H

Pyramid
Lake

Salt
Lake

vid
Basin

Range

No

Sacramento River

Sierra

Nevada

Donner Pa
Lake
Tahoe

EAT

BASIN

UT

Wasatch

Uinta Mts.

Mt. Elbert
14,433 ft.
(4,399 m)

San Juan Mts.

MOUNTAINS

San Joaquin Valley

ges

R.

Mt. Whitney
14,494 ft.
(4,418 m)
▲

Lake
Powell

Colorado River

CO

Sangre de Cristo Mts.

San Central

nt
on

CA

Death
Valley

-282 ft.
(-86 m)

▼

Mojave

Lake
Mead

Grand
Canyon

Colorado

Plateau

So

Desert

AZ

NM

E

Channel
Islands

Salton
Sea

Imperial
Valley

Sonoran
Desert

Baldy Peak ▲
11,403 ft.
(3,476 m)

Guadalupe Peak
8,751 ft.
(2,667 m) ▲

Rio Grande

N
W   E
S

250

500 Miles

UNITED STATES: OVERVIEW

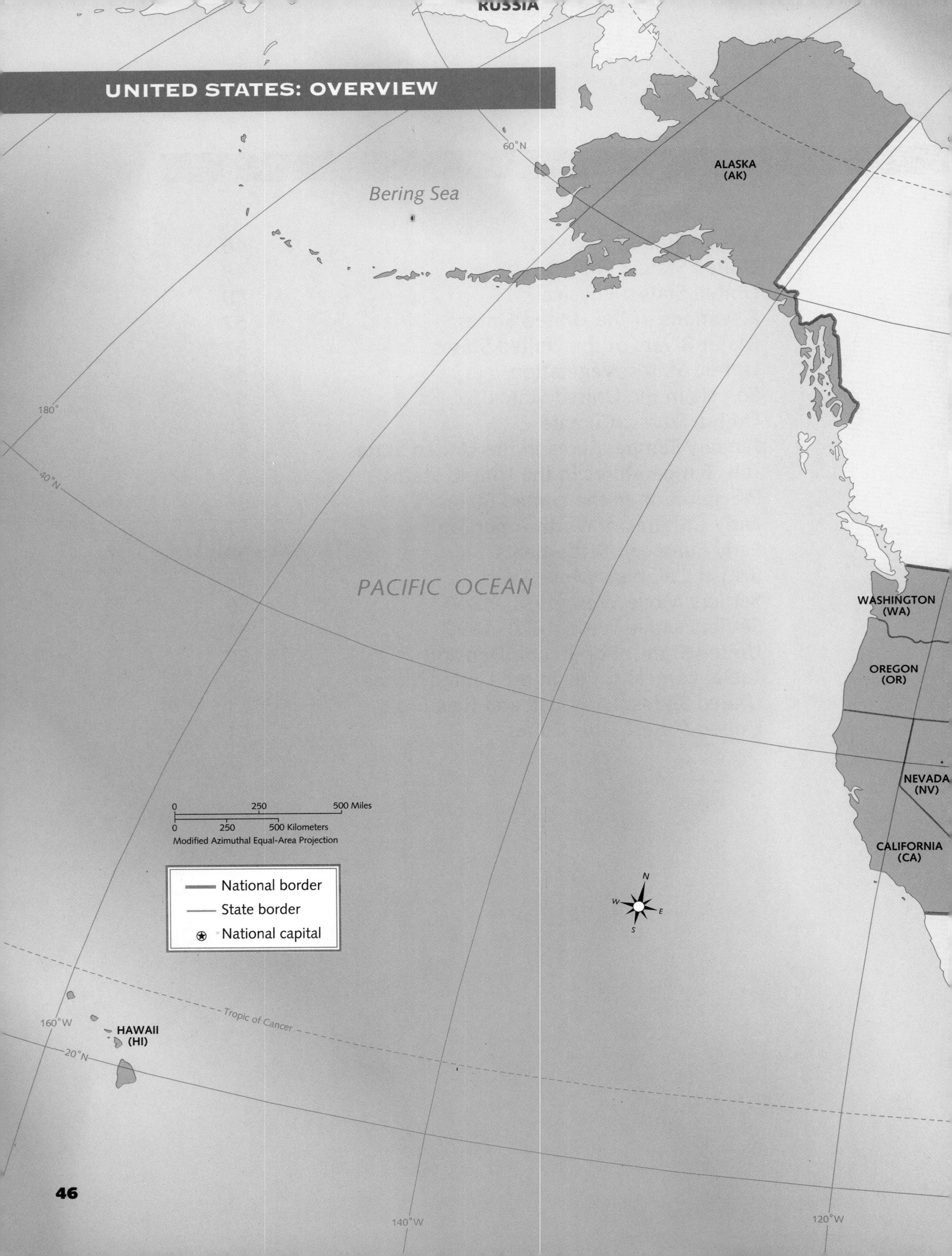
RUSSIA
60° N
Bering Sea
ALASKA (AK)
180°
40° N
PACIFIC OCEAN
WASHINGTON (WA)
OREGON (OR)
NEVADA (NV)
CALIFORNIA (CA)
0 250 500 Miles
0 250 500 Kilometers
Modified Azimuthal Equal-Area Projection
National border
State border
National capital
N
W
E
S
Tropic of Cancer
160° W
HAWAII (HI)
20° N
140° W
120° W

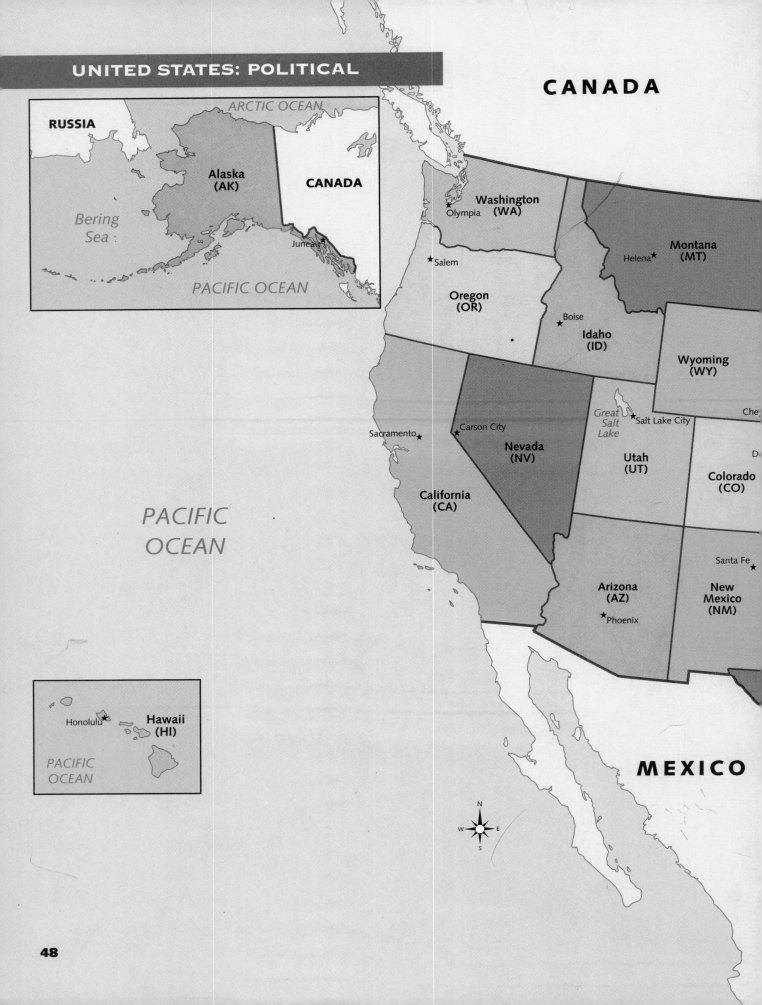

CANADA

RUSSIA

ARCTIC OCEAN

Alaska
(AK)

CANADA

Juneau

Bering
Sea

PACIFIC OCEAN

PACIFIC
OCEAN

★ Olympia

Washington
(WA)

Montana
(MT)

Helena ★

★ Salem

Oregon
(OR)

Boise ★

Idaho
(ID)

Wyoming
(WY)

Che

Great
Salt
Lake

★ Salt Lake City

Sacramento ★

★ Carson City

Nevada
(NV)

Utah
(UT)

Colorado
(CO)

D

California
(CA)

Santa Fe ★

Arizona
(AZ)

New
Mexico
(NM)

★ Phoenix

MEXICO

Honolulu

Hawaii
(HI)

PACIFIC
OCEAN

N
W ★ E
S

CANADA

North Dakota (ND)
★ Bismarck

Minnesota (MN)
St. Paul ★

South Dakota (SD)
Pierre ★

Nebraska (NE)
Lincoln ★

Kansas (KS)
Topeka ★

Oklahoma (OK)
Oklahoma City ★

Texas (TX)
Austin ★

Iowa (IA)
★ Des Moines

Missouri (MO)
Jefferson City ★

Arkansas (AR)
Little Rock ★

Louisiana (LA)
Baton Rouge ★

Wisconsin (WI)
Madison ★

Illinois (IL)
Springfield ★

Lake Superior

Lake Michigan

Michigan (MI)
Lansing ★

Indiana (IN)
Indianapolis ★

Kentucky (KY)
Frankfort ★

Tennessee (TN)
★ Nashville

Mississippi (MS)
Jackson ★

Alabama (AL)
Montgomery ★

Ohio (OH)
Columbus ★

Lake Huron

Lake Erie

Lake Ontario

West Virginia (WV)
Charleston ★

Virginia (VA)
Richmond ★

North Carolina (NC)
Raleigh ★

South Carolina (SC)
Columbia ★

Georgia (GA)
Atlanta ★

Florida (FL)

Tallahassee ★

Pennsylvania (PA)
Harrisburg ★

New York (NY)
Albany ★

Vermont (VT)
Montpelier ★

New Hampshire (NH)
Concord ★

Maine (ME)
Augusta ★

Boston ★
Massachusetts (MA)
Providence ★
Rhode Island (RI)
Hartford ★
Connecticut (CT)

Trenton ★
New Jersey (NJ)

Dover ★
Delaware (DE)

Annapolis ★
Maryland (MD)

Washington, D.C. ✪

ATLANTIC OCEAN

BAHAMAS

Gulf of Mexico

CUBA

CANADA

RUSSIA

ARCTIC OCEAN

Brooks Range

ALASKA

Seward Peninsula

St. Lawrence Island

Yukon River

Arctic Circle

CANADA

Mt. McKinley 20,320 ft. (6,194 m)

Alaska Range

Yukon River

Bering Strait

Bering Sea

Gulf of Alaska

180°

0   250   500 Miles

0   250   500 Kilometers

Aleutian Islands

Kodiak Island

170° E

170° W   160° W   150° W   140° W   130° W

70° N   120° W

60° N

50° N

60° N

Tundra
Evergreen forest
Mixed forest
Grassland
Arid
Mountain
National border
State border
▲ Mountain peak
△ Highest point
▽ Lowest point

PACIFIC OCEAN

Cape Mendocino

Coast Ranges

Cascade Range

Mt. Rainier 14,410 ft. (4,392 m)

Mt. St. Helens 8,364 ft. (2,549 m)

Columbia River

Mt. Hood 11,235 ft. (3,427 m)

WA

OR

Columbia Plateau

Bitterroot Range

ID

Salmon River Mountains

Snake River

MT

Fort Peck Lake

Yellowstone River

Bighorn Mts.

Wind River Range

Teton Range

WY

ROCKY

Sierra Nevada

Sacramento River

San Joaquin

Central Valley

Pyramid Lake

Donner Pass
Lake Tahoe

NV

GREAT BASIN

Great Salt Lake

Wasatch Range

Uinta Mts.

Great Divide Basin

Mt. Elbert 14,433 ft. (4,399 m)

UT

Mt. Whitney 14,495 ft. (4,418 m)

Death Valley -282 ft. (-86 m)

Mojave

Desert

Lake Mead

Grand Canyon

Lake Powell

Colorado River

San Juan Mts.

CO

MOU

Point Conception

CA

Salton Sea

Imperial Valley

Sonoran Desert

Colorado Plateau

AZ

Baldy Peak 11,403 ft. (3,476 m)

NM

Guadalupe Pe 8,749 (2,667

Rio G

Channel Islands

MEXICO

N
W   E
S

HAWAII

160° W   155° W   PACIFIC OCEAN

Kauai

Niihau   Oahu

Molokai

Lanai   Maui

Kahoolawe

Hawaii   20° N

Mauna Kea 13,796 ft. (4,205 m)

0   100   200 Miles

0   100   200 Kilometers

0   250   500 Miles

0   250   500 Kilometers

Albers Equal-Area Projection

100°W · 90°W · 80°W · 70°W

50°N

CANADA

St. Lawrence River

Lake of the Woods

ND

Upper Red Lake
Lower Red Lake
Mesabi
Leech Lake
Mille Lacs Lake

Isle Royale
Lake Superior
Keweenaw Peninsula

Upper Peninsula

Lake Huron

Lake Ontario

Niagara Falls

ME
▲ Mt. Katahdin 5,267 ft. (1,605 m)

VT
NY
Adirondack Mountains
Finger Lakes
Green Mts.
White Mts.
▲ Mt. Washington 6,288 ft. (1,917 m)
Cape Ann

NH
MA
Cape Cod

SD
Lake Oahe

MN
WI
Wisconsin River

MI
Lake St. Clair

Lake Michigan
Lower Peninsula
Lake Winnebago

Lake Erie

PA
Hudson R.
Conn. R.
CT
RI

40°N

Long Island

IA

NE
Sand Hills
North Platte R.
South Platte R.
Platte River

I N T E R I O R   P L A I N S

IL
Illinois River

IN
Wabash River

OH

NJ
Allegheny Mts.
Potomac R.
MD
DE
Delaware Bay

70°N

Smoky Hills

Missouri River

MO

C E N T R A L   P L A I N S

Ohio River

WV
VA
James R.
Cape Charles
Chesapeake Bay

KS

Lake of the Ozarks
Harry S. Truman Reservoir

Lake Barkley

KY
Cumberland Gap
Mt. Mitchell 6,684 ft. (2,037 m) ▲

Roanoke R.
Albemarle Sound
Cape Hatteras

Red Hills

Arkansas River

Mississippi River

NC
Cape Fear River

Smoky Hills

OK
Canadian River
Ouachita

AR

TN

SC
Savannah River
Cape Fear

Red River

A P P A L A C H I A N   M O U N T A I N S

P I E D M O N T   P L A I N

ATLANTIC OCEAN

Llano Estacado

TX
Edwards Plateau

Brazos River
Colorado River

Sabine River
Toledo Bend Reservoir
Sam Rayburn Reservoir

Red River

MS
Tombigbee R.

AL
Alabama R.

Stone Mountain ▲

GA

Okefenokee Swamp

Altamaha R.

30°N

C O A S T A L   P L A I N

Nueces River

Galveston Bay

LA
Lake Pontchartrain

Mobile Bay
Mississippi Delta

St. Johns River
Cape Canaveral

FL
Tampa Bay
Lake Okeechobee

Everglades

B A H A M A S

Cape Sable
Florida Keys

80°W

Gulf of Mexico

CUBA

90°W

51

ELEVATIONS OF THE UNITED STATES

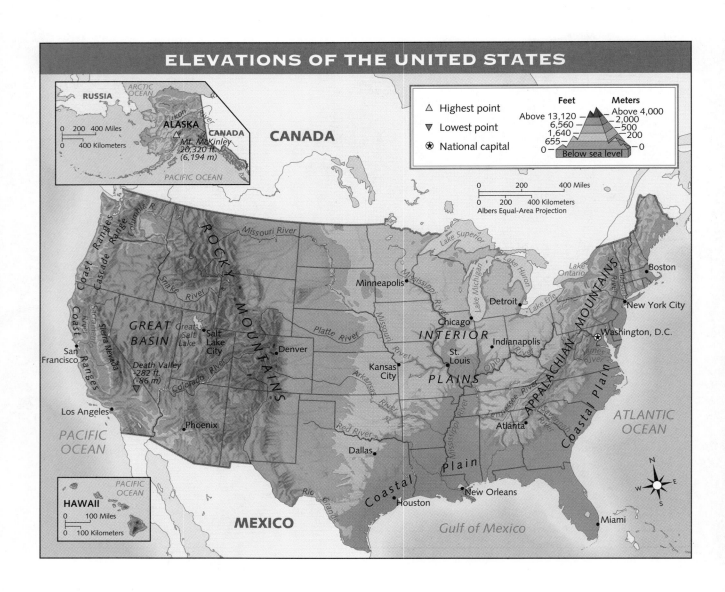

RUSSIA

ARCTIC OCEAN

ALASKA

0   200   400 Miles
0   400 Kilometers

CANADA

Mt. McKinley
20,320 ft.
(6,194 m)

PACIFIC OCEAN

CANADA

	Feet	Meters
△ Highest point		Above 4,000
	Above 13,120	2,000
▽ Lowest point	6,560	500
	1,640	200
⊛ National capital	655	0
	0	

Below sea level

0   200   400 Miles
0   200   400 Kilometers
Albers Equal-Area Projection

Coast Ranges
Cascade Range
Columbia R.
Missouri River
Lake Superior

Minneapolis

Lake Michigan
Lake Huron
Lake Ontario
Lake Erie

Boston

ROCKY MOUNTAINS

Snake River

GREAT BASIN

Great Salt Lake

Salt Lake City

Sierra Nevada

Sacramento R.

Coast Ranges

San Francisco

Death Valley
-282 ft.
(-86 m)

Colorado River

Denver

Platte River

Missouri River

Chicago

Detroit

New York City

INTERIOR

Indianapolis

St. Louis

Washington, D.C.

Ohio R.

APPALACHIAN MOUNTAINS

Hudson River

Kansas City

PLAINS

Arkansas River

Los Angeles

Phoenix

Red River

Tennessee River

Atlanta

Savannah River

Coastal Plain

ATLANTIC OCEAN

PACIFIC OCEAN

Dallas

Rio Grande

Mississippi River

Coastal Plain

New Orleans

Houston

MEXICO

Gulf of Mexico

Miami

PACIFIC OCEAN

HAWAII

0   100 Miles
0   100 Kilometers

N E S W

MAJOR RIVERS OF THE UNITED STATES

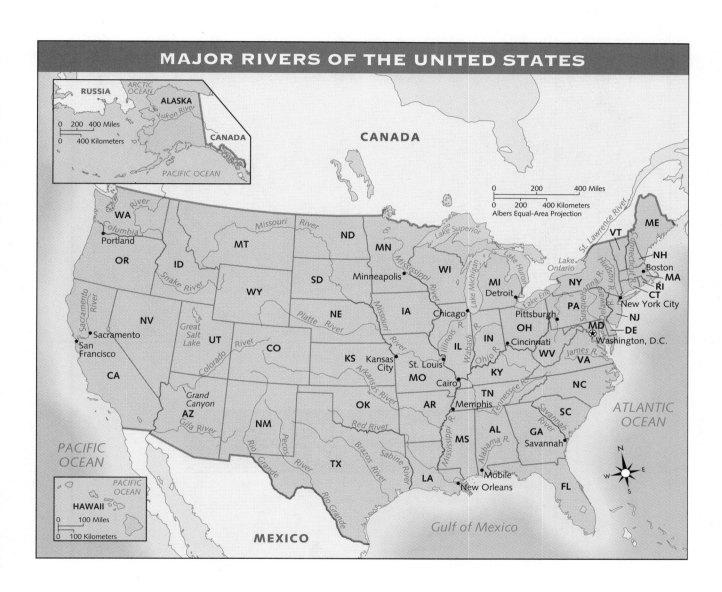

UNITED STATES: VEGETATION

Forest
Grassland
Desert
Tundra

FORESTS IN THE UNITED STATES

Forest

UNITED STATES: CLIMATE

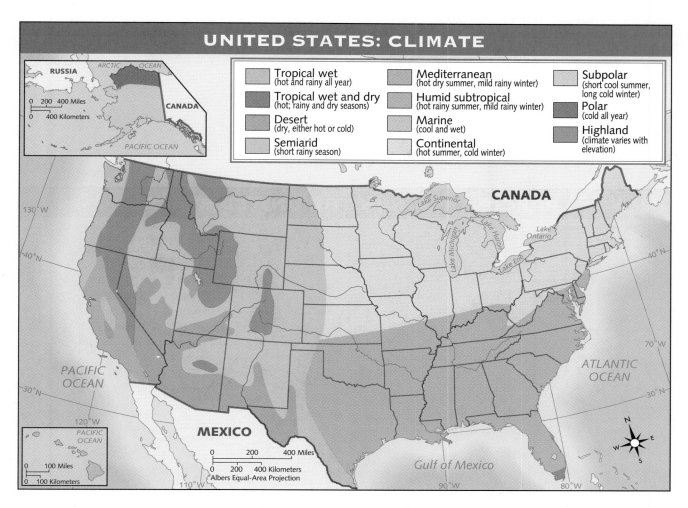

Tropical wet
(hot and rainy all year)

Tropical wet and dry
(hot; rainy and dry seasons)

Desert
(dry, either hot or cold)

Semiarid
(short rainy season)

Mediterranean
(hot dry summer, mild rainy winter)

Humid subtropical
(hot rainy summer, mild rainy winter)

Marine
(cool and wet)

Continental
(hot summer, cold winter)

Subpolar
(short cool summer, long cold winter)

Polar
(cold all year)

Highland
(climate varies with elevation)

JANUARY TEMPERATURES IN THE UNITED STATES

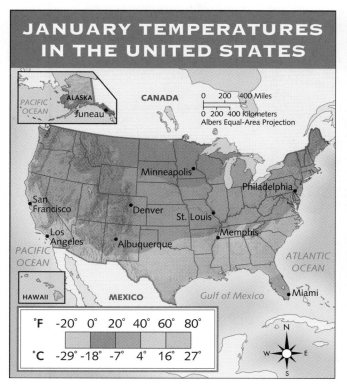

°F -20° 0° 20° 40° 60° 80°

°C -29° -18° -7° 4° 16° 27°

JULY TEMPERATURES IN THE UNITED STATES

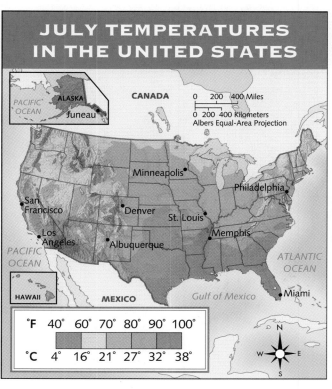

°F 40° 60° 70° 80° 90° 100°

°C 4° 16° 21° 27° 32° 38°

PRECIPITATION IN THE UNITED STATES

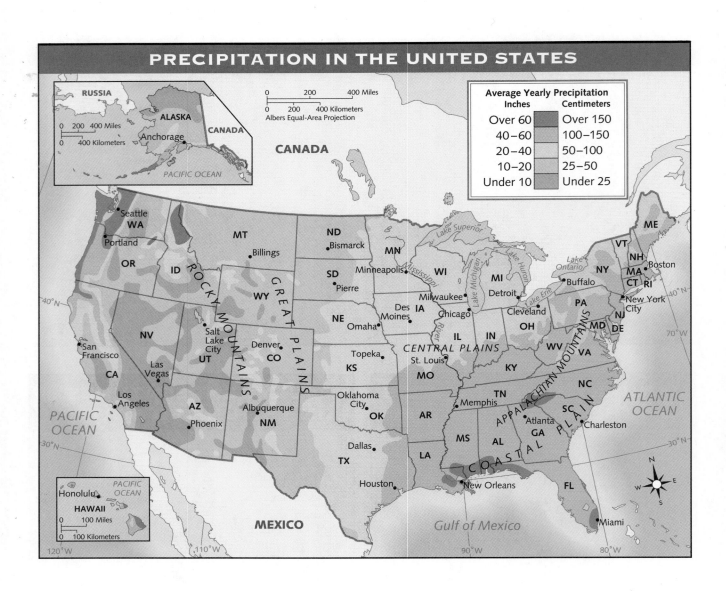

Average Yearly Precipitation

Inches	Centimeters
Over 60	Over 150
40–60	100–150
20–40	50–100
10–20	25–50
Under 10	Under 25

0   200   400 Miles
0   200   400 Kilometers
Albers Equal-Area Projection

RUSSIA

ALASKA

CANADA

Anchorage

PACIFIC OCEAN

0   200   400 Miles
0   400 Kilometers

CANADA

Seattle
WA
Portland
OR
MT
Billings
ID
ROCKY MOUNTAINS
ND
Bismarck
SD
Pierre
MN
Minneapolis
Lake Superior
Mississippi
WI
MI
Milwaukee
Detroit
Lake Michigan
Lake Huron
Lake Ontario
NY
Buffalo
Lake Erie
ME
VT
NH
Boston
MA
CT
RI
New York City

WY
GREAT PLAINS
NE
Omaha
IA
Des Moines
Chicago
IL
IN
OH
Cleveland
PA
APPALACHIAN MOUNTAINS
NJ
MD
DE

NV
Salt Lake City
UT
Denver
CO
Topeka
KS
CENTRAL PLAINS
MO
St. Louis
KY
WV
VA

San Francisco
CA
Las Vegas
Los Angeles
AZ
Phoenix
Albuquerque
NM
Oklahoma City
OK
AR
Memphis
TN
Atlanta
GA
COASTAL PLAIN
NC
SC
Charleston
ATLANTIC OCEAN

PACIFIC OCEAN
Dallas
TX
Houston
LA
MS
AL
New Orleans
FL
Miami

Honolulu
PACIFIC OCEAN
HAWAII
0   100 Miles
0   100 Kilometers

MEXICO

Gulf of Mexico

N
W   E
S

120°W   110°W   90°W   80°W
40°N
30°N
70°W

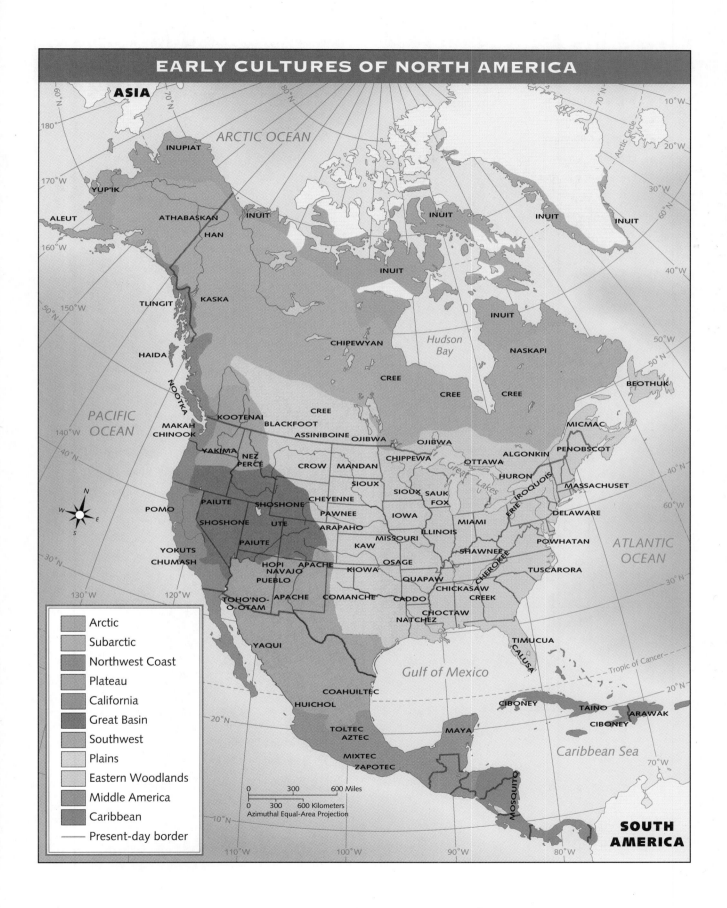

EARLY CULTURES OF NORTH AMERICA

ASIA

ARCTIC OCEAN

INUPIAT

YUP'IK

ALEUT

ATHABASKAN

HAN

INUIT

INUIT

INUIT

INUIT

INUIT

INUIT

TLINGIT

KASKA

CHIPEWYAN

Hudson Bay

NASKAPI

HAIDA

CREE

CREE

CREE

BEOTHUK

PACIFIC OCEAN

NOOTKA

MAKAH

CHINOOK

KOOTENAI

BLACKFOOT

CREE

ASSINIBOINE

OJIBWA

OJIBWA

MICMAC

PENOBSCOT

YAKIMA

NEZ PERCÉ

CROW

MANDAN

CHIPPEWA

OTTAWA

ALGONKIN

HURON

IROQUOIS

MASSACHUSET

POMO

PAIUTE

SHOSHONE

SIOUX

CHEYENNE

SIOUX

SAUK FOX

ERIE

DELAWARE

SHOSHONE

UTE

PAWNEE

IOWA

MIAMI

SHOSHONE

PAIUTE

ARAPAHO

MISSOURI

ILLINOIS

POWHATAN

YOKUTS

KAW

OSAGE

SHAWNEE

CHUMASH

HOPI

NAVAJO

APACHE

KIOWA

QUAPAW

CHEROKEE

TUSCARORA

PUEBLO

CHICKASAW

ATLANTIC OCEAN

TOHO'NO-O-OTAM

APACHE

COMANCHE

CADDO

CREEK

CHOCTAW

NATCHEZ

YAQUI

COAHUILTEC

TIMUCUA

CALUSA

Tropic of Cancer

HUICHOL

Gulf of Mexico

CIBONEY

TAINO

ARAWAK

TOLTEC

AZTEC

MAYA

CIBONEY

MIXTEC

ZAPOTEC

Caribbean Sea

MOSQUITO

SOUTH AMERICA

Legend:
- Arctic
- Subarctic
- Northwest Coast
- Plateau
- California
- Great Basin
- Southwest
- Plains
- Eastern Woodlands
- Middle America
- Caribbean
- Present-day border

0   300   600 Miles
0   300   600 Kilometers
Azimuthal Equal-Area Projection

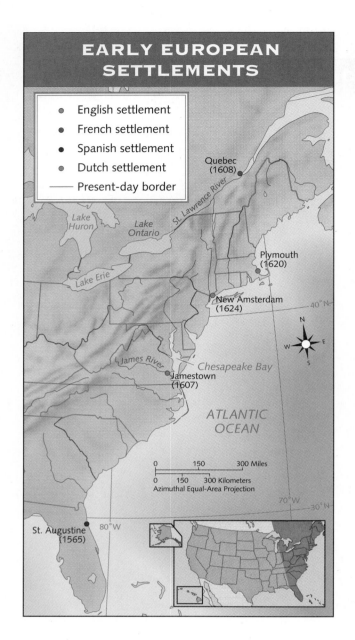

EARLY EUROPEAN SETTLEMENTS

- ● English settlement
- ● French settlement
- ● Spanish settlement
- ● Dutch settlement
- —— Present-day border

Quebec (1608)

Lake Huron

Lake Ontario

St. Lawrence River

Plymouth (1620)

Lake Erie

New Amsterdam (1624)

40°N

James River

Chesapeake Bay

Jamestown (1607)

ATLANTIC OCEAN

0   150   300 Miles
0   150   300 Kilometers
Azimuthal Equal-Area Projection

70°W

30°N

St. Augustine (1565)

80°W

BRITISH COLONISTS MOVE WEST

MAINE (part of Massachusetts)

St. Lawrence River

Lake Champlain

NEW HAMPSHIRE
Portsmouth
Boston
MA Plymouth
Mohawk R.
Connecticut River
Providence
RI Newport

Lake Ontario

NEW YORK
Hudson River
CONNECTICUT

New York City

Lake Erie

PENNSYLVANIA

A P P A L A C H I A N   M O U N T A I N S

NEW JERSEY
Philadelphia
Wilmington
Baltimore
MARYLAND
DELAWARE

Ohio River

VIRGINIA
James River
Williamsburg
Jamestown   Norfolk

Potomac River

NORTH CAROLINA

SOUTH CAROLINA

Savannah River

Augusta

ATLANTIC OCEAN

Charles Towne

GEORGIA

Savannah

0   200   400 Miles
0   200   400 Kilometers
Azimuthal Equal-Area Projection

- ■ Settled by 1660
- ■ Settled by 1700
- ■ Settled by 1760
- —— Present-day border

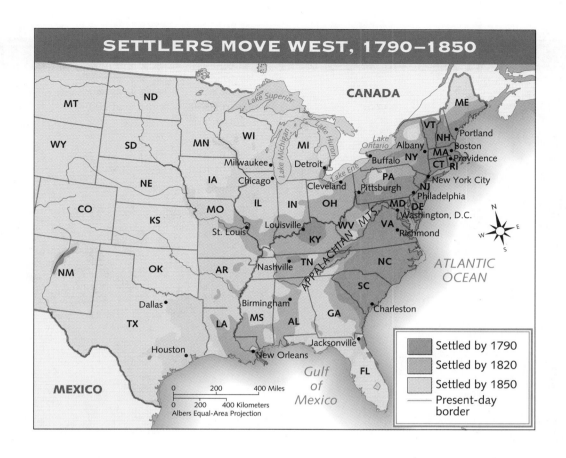

SETTLERS MOVE WEST, 1790–1850

Settled by 1790
Settled by 1820
Settled by 1850
Present-day border

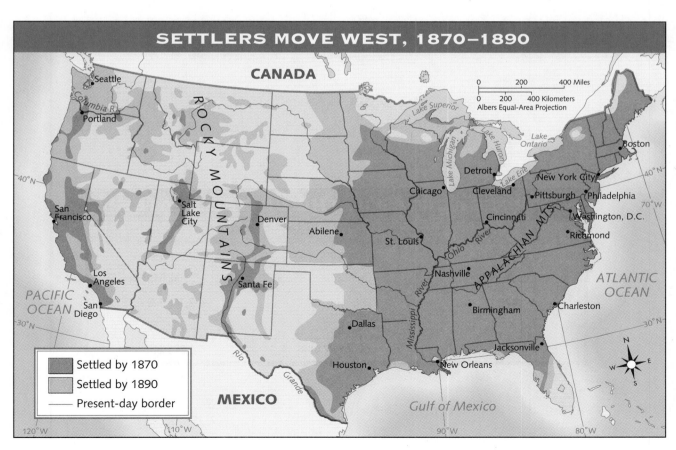

SETTLERS MOVE WEST, 1870–1890

Settled by 1870
Settled by 1890
Present-day border

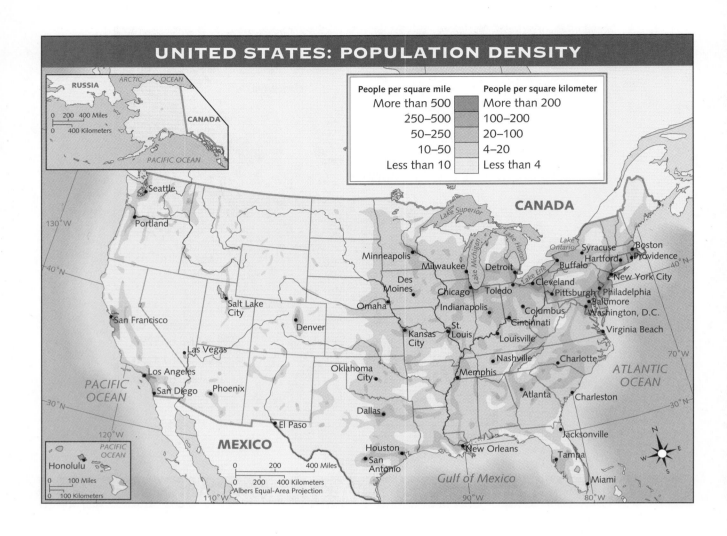

UNITED STATES: POPULATION DENSITY

People per square mile
- More than 500
- 250–500
- 50–250
- 10–50
- Less than 10

People per square kilometer
- More than 200
- 100–200
- 20–100
- 4–20
- Less than 4

Albers Equal-Area Projection

LARGEST CITIES IN THE UNITED STATES

CITY	STATE	POPULATION*
New York	New York	7,333,253
Los Angeles	California	3,448,613
Chicago	Illinois	2,731,743
Houston	Texas	1,702,086
Philadelphia	Pennsylvania	1,524,249

*The most recent figures available

UNITED STATES: LAND USE AND RESOURCES

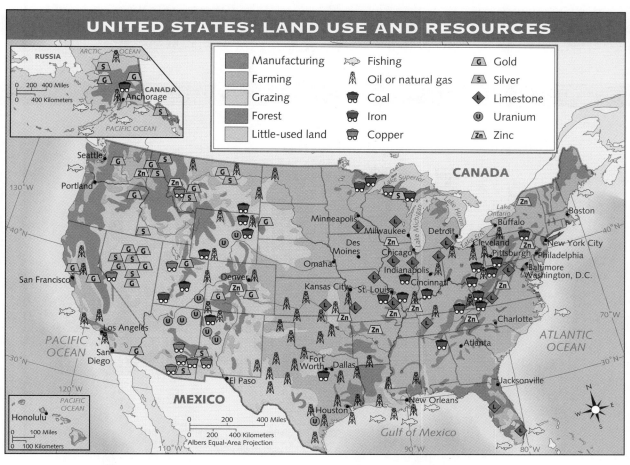

Legend:
- Manufacturing
- Farming
- Grazing
- Forest
- Little-used land
- Fishing
- Oil or natural gas
- Coal
- Iron
- Copper
- Gold (G)
- Silver (S)
- Limestone (L)
- Uranium (U)
- Zinc (Zn)

UNITED STATES TIME ZONES

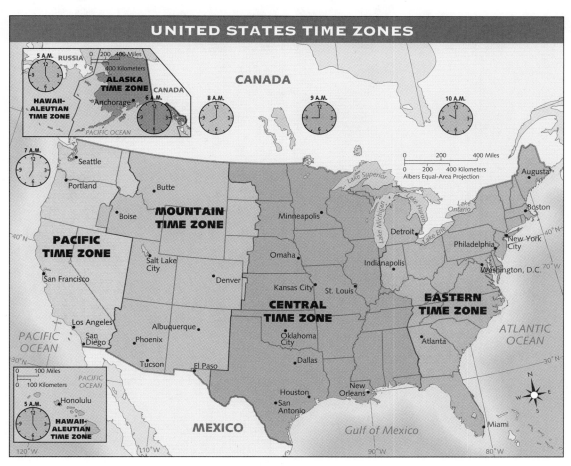

United States Regions

UNITED STATES: REGIONS

CANADA

RUSSIA

ARCTIC OCEAN

70°N

120°W

ALASKA

Arctic Circle

170°E

60°N

CANADA

Yukon River

Fairbanks

Bering Sea

Anchorage

60°N

180°

0   250   500 Miles

0   250   500 Kilometers

Juneau

PACIFIC OCEAN

50°N

170°W   160°W   150°W   140°W   130°W

130°W   120°W   110°W

Seattle
Tacoma
Olympia   Spokane

WASHINGTON

Portland   Columbia River
Salem

Eugene

OREGON

Great Falls
Helena   **MONTANA**
Billings

IDAHO

40°N

Boise

Snake River

WYOMING

Pocatello

Casper

Ogden   Salt Lake City   Che

NEVADA

Reno   Great Salt Lake   Provo

Sacramento   Carson City

San Francisco   Oakland
San Jose

UTAH

PACIFIC OCEAN

Fresno

CALIFORNIA

Las Vegas

D

Colorado River

Co

COLORADO

Bakersfield

30°N

Flagstaff

Santa Fe
Albuquerque

Los Angeles   San Bernardino

ARIZONA

NEW MEXICO

San Diego

Phoenix

Ro

130°W

Tucson

El Pas

	Northeast	⊛	National capital
	Southeast	★	State capital
	Middle West	•	Major city
	Southwest		National border
	West		State border

Rio U

MEXICO

N
W   E
S

160°W   PACIFIC OCEAN   155°W

Honolulu

HAWAII

Hilo

20°N

0   125   250 Miles

0   125   250 Kilometers

0   250   500 Miles

0   250   500 Kilometers

Albers Equal-Area Projection

20°N

120°W   110°W

64

REGION

Did You Know?

There are 11 states in the Northeast. Of those states, 6 are known together as the New England states. The other 5 states are known as the Middle Atlantic states. The nation's capital, Washington, D.C., is also a part of the Northeast.

STATE	CAPITAL	NICKNAME	POPULATION*
THE NEW ENGLAND STATES			
Connecticut (CT)	Hartford	Constitution State	3,269,000
Maine (ME)	Augusta	Pine Tree State	1,242,000
Massachusetts (MA)	Boston	Bay State	6,118,000
New Hampshire (NH)	Concord	Granite State	1,172,000
Rhode Island (RI)	Providence	Ocean State	987,000
Vermont (VT)	Montpelier	Green Mountain State	588,000
THE MIDDLE ATLANTIC STATES			
Delaware (DE)	Dover	First State	731,000
Maryland (MD)	Annapolis	Old Line State	5,094,000
New Jersey (NJ)	Trenton	Garden State	8,052,000
New York (NY)	Albany	Empire State	18,137,000
Pennsylvania (PA)	Harrisburg	Keystone State	12,019,000

*The most recent figures available

TEN LARGEST CITIES

1. New York, New York
2. Philadelphia, Pennsylvania
3. Baltimore, Maryland
4. Washington, D.C.
5. Boston, Massachusetts
6. Pittsburgh, Pennsylvania
7. Buffalo, New York
8. Newark, New Jersey
9. Rochester, New York
10. Jersey City, New Jersey

LEADING PRODUCTS AND RESOURCES

Farming:
Apples, beef cattle, blueberries, cranberries, dairy cows, potatoes, poultry
Fishing:
Clams, crabs, fish, lobsters, scallops
Manufacturing:
Chemicals, clothing, dairy products, electrical equipment, lumber, maple syrup, medicines, paper products, plastics, printed materials, processed foods
Mining:
Coal, gravel, iron, natural gas, oil, sand, stone, zinc

The Verrazano-Narrows Bridge, in New York, has the longest span of any bridge in the United States—4,260 feet (1,298 m).

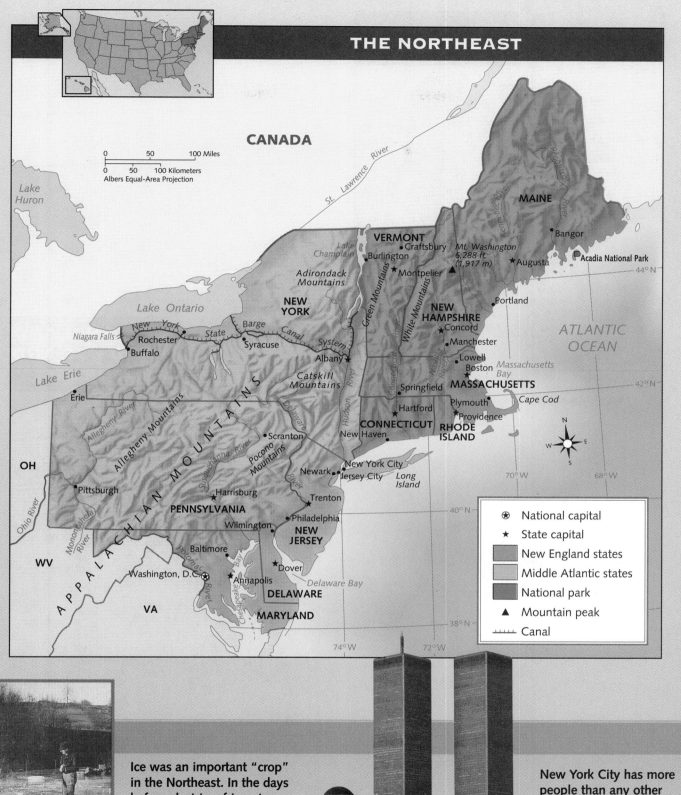

CANADA

0   50   100 Miles
0 50 100 Kilometers
Albers Equal-Area Projection

Lake Huron

Lake Ontario

Lake Erie

Niagara Falls

St. Lawrence River

MAINE

Bangor

VERMONT

Craftsbury

Lake Champlain

Burlington

Adirondack Mountains

NEW YORK

Montpelier

Mt. Washington 6,288 ft. (1,917 m)

Augusta

Acadia National Park

NEW HAMPSHIRE

Concord

Portland

Manchester

Green Mountains

White Mountains

Rochester

New York State

Barge

Canal

System

Syracuse

Albany

Lowell

Boston

ATLANTIC OCEAN

Buffalo

Massachusetts Bay

Catskill Mountains

Hudson River

Springfield

MASSACHUSETTS

Erie

Hartford

Plymouth

Cape Cod

OH

Allegheny River

Allegheny Mountains

Delaware River

Scranton

CONNECTICUT

Providence

RHODE ISLAND

New Haven

Pittsburgh

Susquehanna River

Pocono Mountains

Newark

New York City

Jersey City

Long Island

APPALACHIAN MOUNTAINS

Harrisburg

Trenton

N
W   E
S

70° W

68° W

WV

Monongahela River

PENNSYLVANIA

Philadelphia

Wilmington

NEW JERSEY

Baltimore

Dover

Washington, D.C.

Annapolis

Delaware Bay

VA

Chesapeake Bay

DELAWARE

MARYLAND

Ohio River

Potomac River

74° W

72° W

44° N

42° N

40° N

38° N

⊛ National capital
★ State capital
■ New England states
■ Middle Atlantic states
■ National park
▲ Mountain peak
⊥⊥⊥ Canal

Ice was an important "crop" in the Northeast. In the days before electric refrigerators, ice was used to cool food. It was cut from frozen rivers and lakes and shipped to places all over the United States. In 1890, 3 million tons were cut in the state of Maine alone.

New York City has more people than any other city in the United States. More than 7 million people live there.

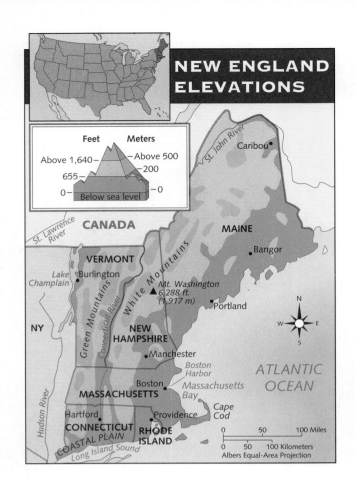

NEW ENGLAND ELEVATIONS

Feet   Meters
Above 1,640 — Above 500
655 — 200
0 — 0
Below sea level

St. John River
Caribou
St. Lawrence River
CANADA
MAINE
Bangor
VERMONT
Burlington
Lake Champlain
White Mountains
Green Mountains
Connecticut River
Mt. Washington
6,288 ft.
(1,917 m)
Portland
NY
NEW HAMPSHIRE
Manchester
Boston Harbor
ATLANTIC OCEAN
Hudson River
MASSACHUSETTS
Boston
Massachusetts Bay
Cape Cod
Hartford
Providence
CONNECTICUT
RHODE ISLAND
COASTAL PLAIN
Long Island Sound

N W E S

0   50   100 Miles
0   50   100 Kilometers
Albers Equal-Area Projection

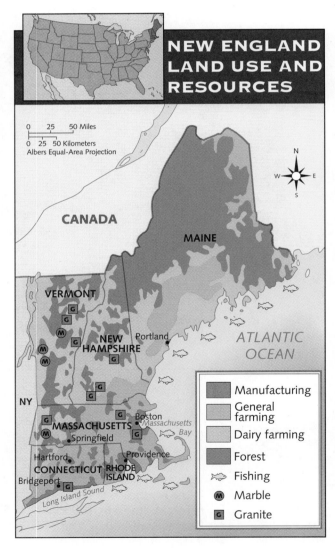

NEW ENGLAND LAND USE AND RESOURCES

0   25   50 Miles
0   25   50 Kilometers
Albers Equal-Area Projection

CANADA
MAINE
VERMONT
NEW HAMPSHIRE
Portland
ATLANTIC OCEAN
NY
MASSACHUSETTS
Springfield
Boston
Massachusetts Bay
Hartford
Providence
CONNECTICUT
RHODE ISLAND
Bridgeport
Long Island Sound

N W E S

Manufacturing
General farming
Dairy farming
Forest
Fishing
Ⓜ Marble
Ⓖ Granite

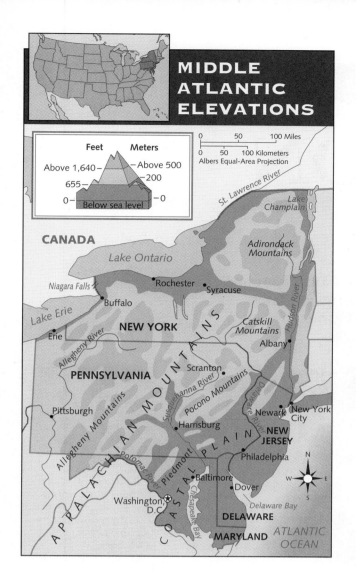

MIDDLE ATLANTIC ELEVATIONS

Feet **Meters**

Above 1,640 — — Above 500

655 — — 200

0 — — 0

Below sea level

0   50   100 Miles

0   50   100 Kilometers

Albers Equal-Area Projection

St. Lawrence River

Lake Champlain

CANADA

Lake Ontario

Adirondack Mountains

Niagara Falls

Rochester

Syracuse

Buffalo

Lake Erie

Erie

NEW YORK

Catskill Mountains

Hudson River

Albany

Allegheny River

APPALACHIAN MOUNTAINS

Scranton

PENNSYLVANIA

Susquehanna River

Pocono Mountains

Delaware River

Newark

New York City

Pittsburgh

Allegheny Mountains

Harrisburg

NEW JERSEY

Philadelphia

Potomac River

Piedmont

COASTAL PLAIN

Baltimore

Dover

Washington, D.C.

Chesapeake Bay

Delaware Bay

DELAWARE

MARYLAND

ATLANTIC OCEAN

N W E S

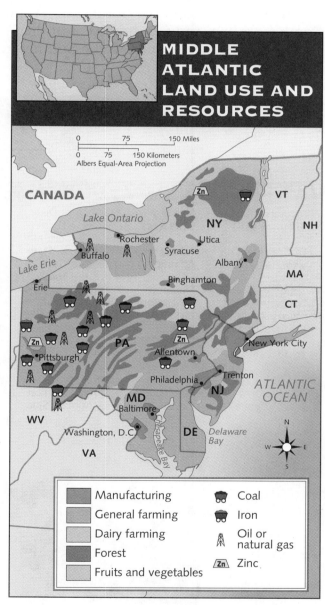

MIDDLE ATLANTIC LAND USE AND RESOURCES

0   75   150 Miles

0   75   150 Kilometers

Albers Equal-Area Projection

CANADA

Lake Ontario

Zn

VT

NY

NH

Rochester

Utica

Lake Erie

Buffalo

Syracuse

Albany

MA

Erie

Binghamton

CT

New York City

Zn

Zn

PA

Allentown

Pittsburgh

Trenton

Philadelphia

NJ

WV

MD

Baltimore

Washington, D.C.

DE

Delaware Bay

ATLANTIC OCEAN

VA

N W E S

Manufacturing		Coal
General farming		Iron
Dairy farming		Oil or natural gas
Forest		Zn Zinc
Fruits and vegetables		

REGION

Did You Know?

There are 12 states in the Southeast. Virginia, North Carolina, South Carolina, and Georgia are 4 of the 13 original states. Georgia is the largest state in the Southeast. Florida, however, has the most people.

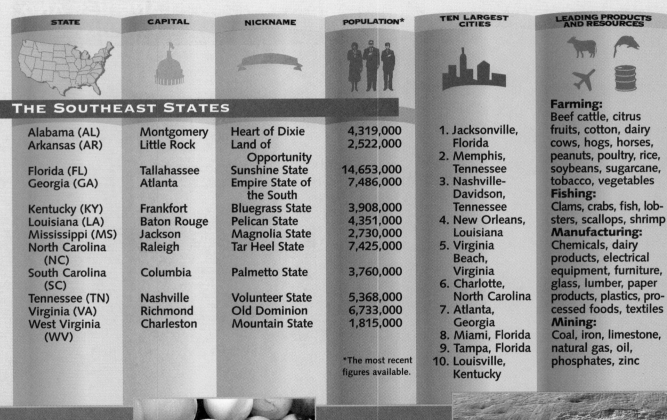

STATE	CAPITAL	NICKNAME	POPULATION*	TEN LARGEST CITIES	LEADING PRODUCTS AND RESOURCES

THE SOUTHEAST STATES

STATE	CAPITAL	NICKNAME	POPULATION*
Alabama (AL)	Montgomery	Heart of Dixie	4,319,000
Arkansas (AR)	Little Rock	Land of Opportunity	2,522,000
Florida (FL)	Tallahassee	Sunshine State	14,653,000
Georgia (GA)	Atlanta	Empire State of the South	7,486,000
Kentucky (KY)	Frankfort	Bluegrass State	3,908,000
Louisiana (LA)	Baton Rouge	Pelican State	4,351,000
Mississippi (MS)	Jackson	Magnolia State	2,730,000
North Carolina (NC)	Raleigh	Tar Heel State	7,425,000
South Carolina (SC)	Columbia	Palmetto State	3,760,000
Tennessee (TN)	Nashville	Volunteer State	5,368,000
Virginia (VA)	Richmond	Old Dominion	6,733,000
West Virginia (WV)	Charleston	Mountain State	1,815,000

*The most recent figures available.

TEN LARGEST CITIES
1. Jacksonville, Florida
2. Memphis, Tennessee
3. Nashville-Davidson, Tennessee
4. New Orleans, Louisiana
5. Virginia Beach, Virginia
6. Charlotte, North Carolina
7. Atlanta, Georgia
8. Miami, Florida
9. Tampa, Florida
10. Louisville, Kentucky

LEADING PRODUCTS AND RESOURCES

Farming:
Beef cattle, citrus fruits, cotton, dairy cows, hogs, horses, peanuts, poultry, rice, soybeans, sugarcane, tobacco, vegetables
Fishing:
Clams, crabs, fish, lobsters, scallops, shrimp
Manufacturing:
Chemicals, dairy products, electrical equipment, furniture, glass, lumber, paper products, plastics, processed foods, textiles
Mining:
Coal, iron, limestone, natural gas, oil, phosphates, zinc

Most of the glass marbles manufactured in the United States are made in West Virginia.

The largest sculpture in the world is carved on the face of Stone Mountain, in Georgia. Stone Mountain is the largest mass of granite in North America.

THE SOUTHEAST

State / Places on map:

KS · MO · IL · IN · OH · PA · NJ · MD · DE

Wheeling

WEST VIRGINIA
★ Charleston
Huntington

Shenandoah National Park

VIRGINIA
★ Richmond
Lynchburg
Roanoke
Virginia Beach
Norfolk
Dismal Swamp
Chesapeake Bay
Outer Banks

Louisville
Frankfort ★
Lexington
Owensboro

KENTUCKY

Mammoth Cave National Park

Cumberland Gap

Jonesborough
Greensboro
Raleigh ★

Nashville ★
Knoxville
Great Smoky Mountains National Park
Asheville
Canton

NORTH CAROLINA

Mt. Mitchell
6,684 ft. (2,037 m) ▲

Charlotte
Cape Hatteras

ARKANSAS
Fort Smith
Little Rock ★
Hot Springs National Park

Arkansas River

TENNESSEE
Memphis
Chattanooga
Huntsville

Greenville

SOUTH CAROLINA
Columbia ★

Wilmington
Cape Fear

COASTAL PLAIN

Atlanta
Stone Mountain ▲
GEORGIA
Macon
Charleston

Birmingham

MISSISSIPPI
ALABAMA
Montgomery ★
Columbus

Savannah
Hilton Head Island

Shreveport
Monroe
Jackson ★

Okefenokee Swamp

ATLANTIC OCEAN

TX

Red River
Sabine River
Pearl River
Tombigbee River
Alabama River
Chattahoochee River
Ocmulgee River
Altamaha River
Savannah River

LOUISIANA
Baton Rouge ★
Lake Charles
Biloxi
Mobile
Pensacola

Tallahassee ★

FLORIDA

Jacksonville
St. Augustine
Daytona Beach

New Orleans
Mississippi Delta

COASTAL PLAIN

Orlando
Cape Canaveral

St. Johns River

Gulf of Mexico

Tampa
St. Petersburg

Lake Okeechobee

West Palm Beach

Big Cypress Swamp
Everglades

Miami
Biscayne National Park

Everglades National Park

Florida Keys

95°W · 90°W · 85°W · 80°W · 75°W · 70°W
35°N · 30°N · 25°N

Legend:
★ State capital
— State boundary
▨ National park
▲ Mountain peak
▧ Swamp

0   150   300 Miles
0   150   300 Kilometers
Albers Equal-Area Projection

Mammoth Cave, in Kentucky, is part of the world's largest known cave system.

St. Augustine, Florida, is the oldest permanent settlement built by Europeans in what is today the United States. It was settled by the Spanish in 1565.

The manatee is an endangered sea mammal found near Florida's coasts.

71

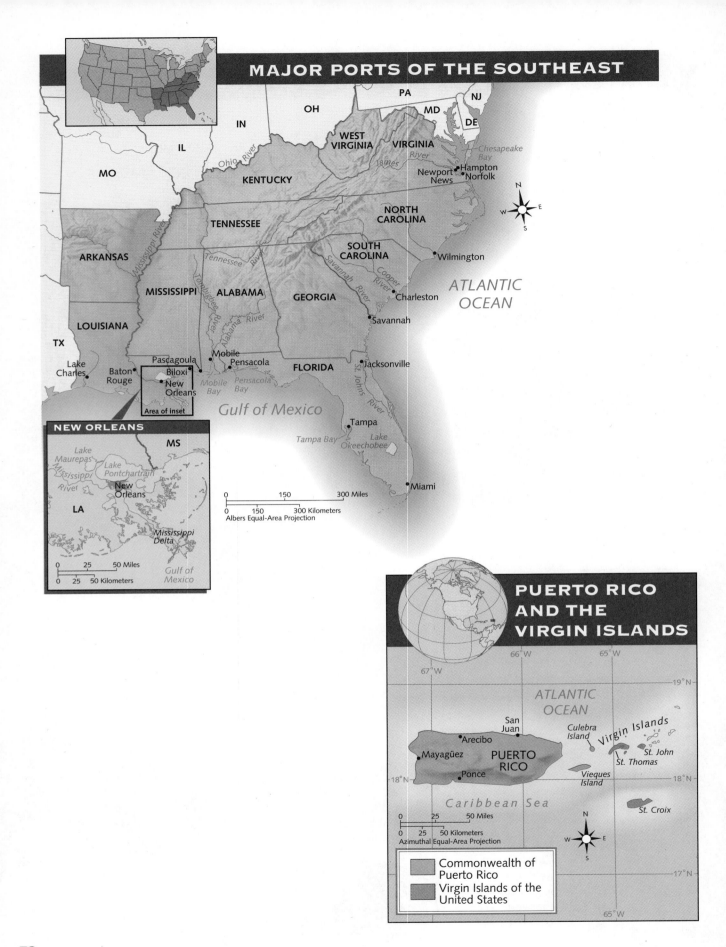

PA

NJ

OH

MD

DE

WEST VIRGINIA

VIRGINIA

Chesapeake Bay

Ohio River

James River

Newport News

Hampton

Norfolk

IN

IL

MO

KENTUCKY

N

W E

S

NORTH CAROLINA

TENNESSEE

Wilmington

ARKANSAS

Mississippi River

Tennessee River

SOUTH CAROLINA

Savannah River

Cooper River

Charleston

ATLANTIC OCEAN

MISSISSIPPI

ALABAMA

Tombigbee River

GEORGIA

Savannah

LOUISIANA

Alabama River

TX

Lake Charles

Baton Rouge

Pascagoula

Biloxi

New Orleans

Area of inset

Mobile

Pensacola

Mobile Bay

Pensacola Bay

FLORIDA

Jacksonville

St. Johns River

Gulf of Mexico

Tampa

Tampa Bay

Lake Okeechobee

Miami

NEW ORLEANS

MS

Lake Maurepas

Lake Pontchartrain

Mississippi River

New Orleans

LA

Mississippi Delta

Gulf of Mexico

0   25   50 Miles

0   25   50 Kilometers

0   150   300 Miles

0   150   300 Kilometers

Albers Equal-Area Projection

PUERTO RICO AND THE VIRGIN ISLANDS

66°W

65°W

19°N

ATLANTIC OCEAN

67°W

San Juan

Culebra Island

Virgin Islands

Arecibo

PUERTO RICO

St. John

Mayagüez

St. Thomas

Ponce

Vieques Island

18°N

18°N

Caribbean Sea

St. Croix

0   25   50 Miles

0   25   50 Kilometers

Azimuthal Equal-Area Projection

N

W E

S

17°N

65°W

Commonwealth of Puerto Rico

Virgin Islands of the United States

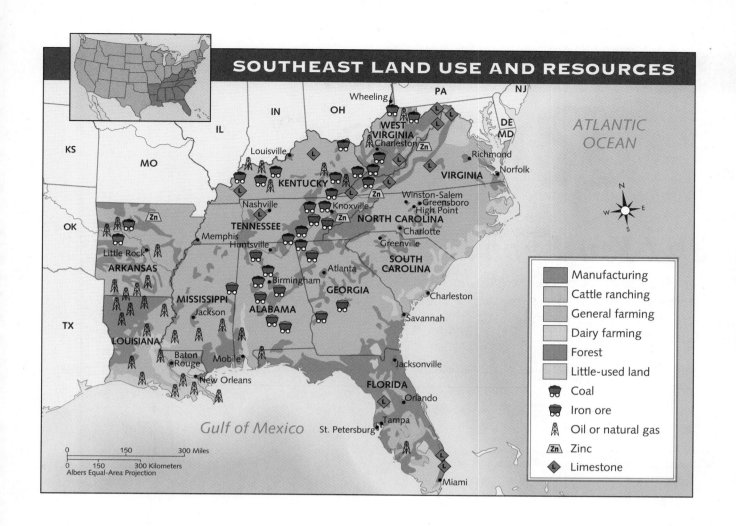

SOUTHEAST LAND USE AND RESOURCES

KS
MO
IL
IN
OH
PA
NJ
Wheeling
WEST VIRGINIA
Charleston
DE
MD
Richmond
VIRGINIA
Norfolk
ATLANTIC OCEAN
Louisville
KENTUCKY
Winston-Salem
Greensboro
High Point
Knoxville
NORTH CAROLINA
Nashville
Charlotte
TENNESSEE
Greenville
Memphis
Huntsville
SOUTH CAROLINA
OK
Little Rock
ARKANSAS
Atlanta
Birmingham
GEORGIA
Charleston
MISSISSIPPI
ALABAMA
Savannah
TX
Jackson
LOUISIANA
Baton Rouge
Mobile
Jacksonville
New Orleans
FLORIDA
Orlando
Gulf of Mexico
Tampa
St. Petersburg
Miami

N
W E
S

	Manufacturing
	Cattle ranching
	General farming
	Dairy farming
	Forest
	Little-used land
Coal	
Iron ore	
Oil or natural gas	
Zn	Zinc
L	Limestone

0   150   300 Miles
0   150   300 Kilometers
Albers Equal-Area Projection

LEADING CHICKEN-PRODUCING STATES

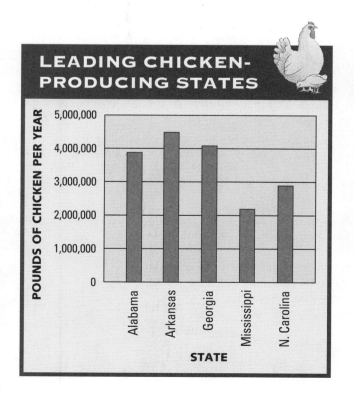

POUNDS OF CHICKEN PER YEAR

5,000,000
4,000,000
3,000,000
2,000,000
1,000,000
0

Alabama
Arkansas
Georgia
Mississippi
N. Carolina

STATE

TENNESSEE VALLEY AUTHORITY

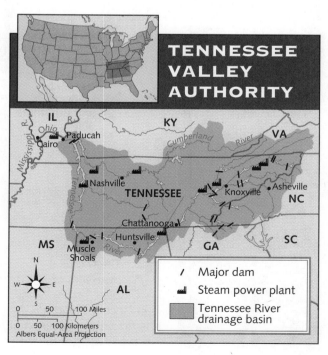

IL
KY
VA
Ohio R.
Paducah
Cairo
Cumberland River
Mississippi R.
Nashville
TENNESSEE
Knoxville
Asheville
NC
Tennessee R.
Chattanooga
Huntsville
SC
MS
Muscle Shoals
GA
AL
Tennessee River

N
W E
S

/	Major dam
	Steam power plant
	Tennessee River drainage basin

0   50   100 Miles
0   50   100 Kilometers
Albers Equal-Area Projection

REGION

Did You Know?

Twelve states make up the Middle West. Sometimes those states are divided into two smaller regions—the Plains states and the Great Lakes states. All six Great Lakes states border a Great Lake.

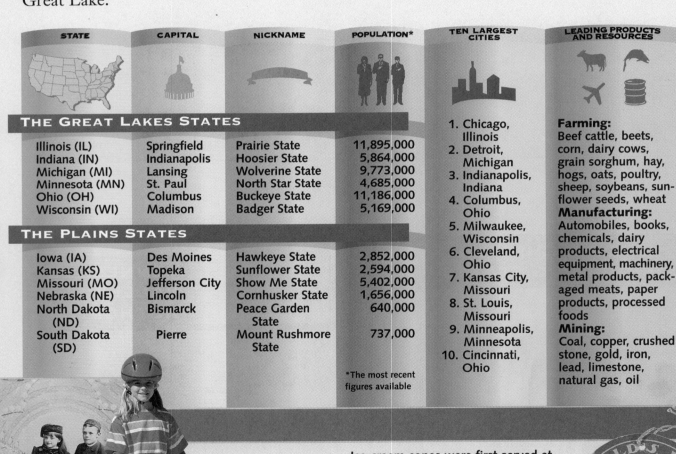

STATE	CAPITAL	NICKNAME	POPULATION*	TEN LARGEST CITIES	LEADING PRODUCTS AND RESOURCES
THE GREAT LAKES STATES				1. Chicago, Illinois	**Farming:** Beef cattle, beets, corn, dairy cows, grain sorghum, hay, hogs, oats, poultry, sheep, soybeans, sunflower seeds, wheat
Illinois (IL)	Springfield	Prairie State	11,895,000	2. Detroit, Michigan	
Indiana (IN)	Indianapolis	Hoosier State	5,864,000	3. Indianapolis, Indiana	
Michigan (MI)	Lansing	Wolverine State	9,773,000	4. Columbus, Ohio	**Manufacturing:** Automobiles, books, chemicals, dairy products, electrical equipment, machinery, metal products, packaged meats, paper products, processed foods
Minnesota (MN)	St. Paul	North Star State	4,685,000	5. Milwaukee, Wisconsin	
Ohio (OH)	Columbus	Buckeye State	11,186,000	6. Cleveland, Ohio	
Wisconsin (WI)	Madison	Badger State	5,169,000	7. Kansas City, Missouri	
THE PLAINS STATES				8. St. Louis, Missouri	
Iowa (IA)	Des Moines	Hawkeye State	2,852,000	9. Minneapolis, Minnesota	**Mining:** Coal, copper, crushed stone, gold, iron, lead, limestone, natural gas, oil
Kansas (KS)	Topeka	Sunflower State	2,594,000	10. Cincinnati, Ohio	
Missouri (MO)	Jefferson City	Show Me State	5,402,000		
Nebraska (NE)	Lincoln	Cornhusker State	1,656,000		
North Dakota (ND)	Bismarck	Peace Garden State	640,000		
South Dakota (SD)	Pierre	Mount Rushmore State	737,000		

*The most recent figures available

The National Museum of Roller Skating is in Lincoln, Nebraska. It is the only museum in the world just for roller skating.

Ice-cream cones were first served at the 1904 Louisiana Purchase Exposition World's Fair in St. Louis, Missouri.

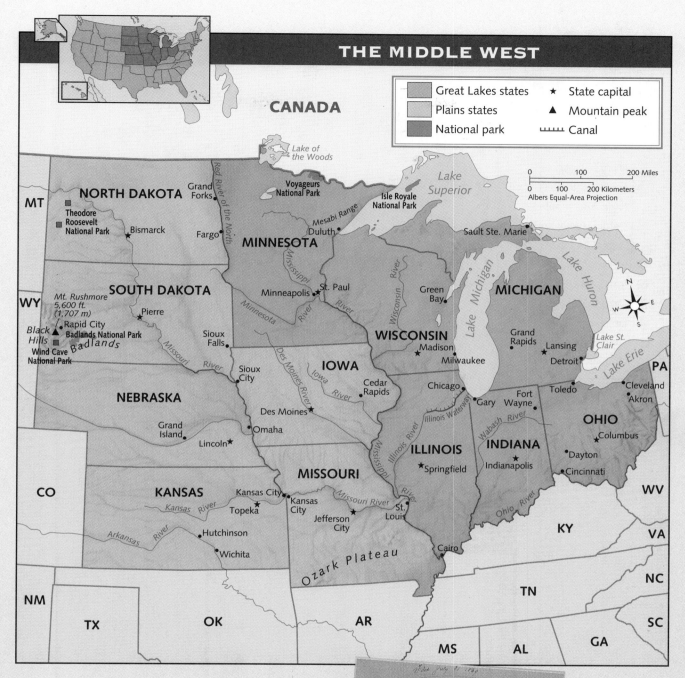

CANADA

Legend

Great Lakes states		★	State capital
Plains states		▲	Mountain peak
National park		⊔⊔⊔	Canal

0   100   200 Miles
0   100   200 Kilometers
Albers Equal-Area Projection

Lake of the Woods

NORTH DAKOTA
Grand Forks
MT
Theodore Roosevelt National Park
Bismarck ★
Fargo

Voyageurs National Park
Red River of the North

Lake Superior

Isle Royale National Park

Mesabi Range
Duluth

Sault Ste. Marie

MINNESOTA
Mississippi River

WY
SOUTH DAKOTA
Mt. Rushmore 5,600 ft. (1,707 m)
Pierre ★
Black Hills
▲ Rapid City
Badlands National Park
Badlands
Wind Cave National Park
Minnesota River
Minneapolis
St. Paul ★

Green Bay

Lake Michigan

MICHIGAN
Grand Rapids
Lansing ★
Detroit
Lake Huron
Lake St. Clair
Lake Erie

WISCONSIN
Wisconsin River
Madison ★
Milwaukee

Sioux Falls

NEBRASKA
Missouri River
Sioux City

IOWA
Des Moines River
Iowa River
Cedar Rapids
Des Moines ★

Chicago
Gary
Fort Wayne
Illinois Waterway

Toledo
PA
Cleveland
Akron

Grand Island
Omaha
Lincoln ★

Illinois River
Wabash River

OHIO
Columbus ★
Dayton
Cincinnati

KANSAS
Kansas City
Topeka ★
Hutchinson
Wichita
Kansas River
Arkansas River

Kansas City
Jefferson City

MISSOURI
Missouri River
Mississippi River
St. Louis

ILLINOIS
Springfield ★

INDIANA
Indianapolis ★

WV

CO

Ohio River
Cairo
Ozark Plateau

KY

VA

NM

TX
OK
AR
TN
NC
SC

MS
AL
GA

SIWINOWE
Kesibwi.
PALAKO WAHOSTOTA NAKOTE KESIBO.—WISELIBI. 1841.
NOVEMBER. 1841.   BAPTIST MISSION PRESS
J. LYKINS EDITOR.

The first newspaper in North America to be printed entirely in an Indian language was the *Siwinowe Kesibwi*, or "Shawnee Sun." It was first printed in Kansas in 1835.

In 1869 the Cincinnati Red Stockings, now the Cincinnati Reds, became the first professional baseball team.

MIDDLE WEST LAND USE AND RESOURCES

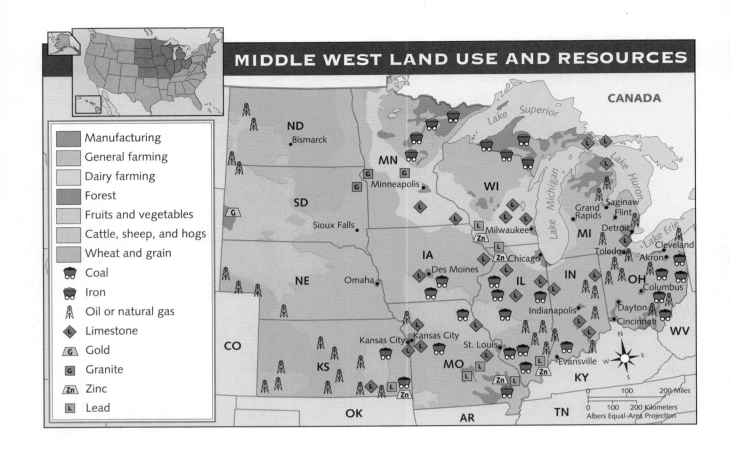

Manufacturing
General farming
Dairy farming
Forest
Fruits and vegetables
Cattle, sheep, and hogs
Wheat and grain
Coal
Iron
Oil or natural gas
Limestone
Gold
Granite
Zinc
Lead

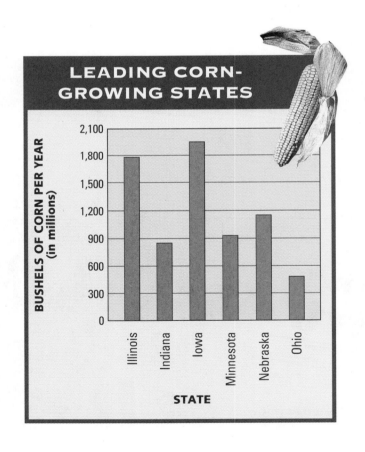

LEADING CORN-GROWING STATES

BUSHELS OF CORN PER YEAR (in millions)

2,100
1,800
1,500
1,200
900
600
300
0

Illinois · Indiana · Iowa · Minnesota · Nebraska · Ohio

STATE

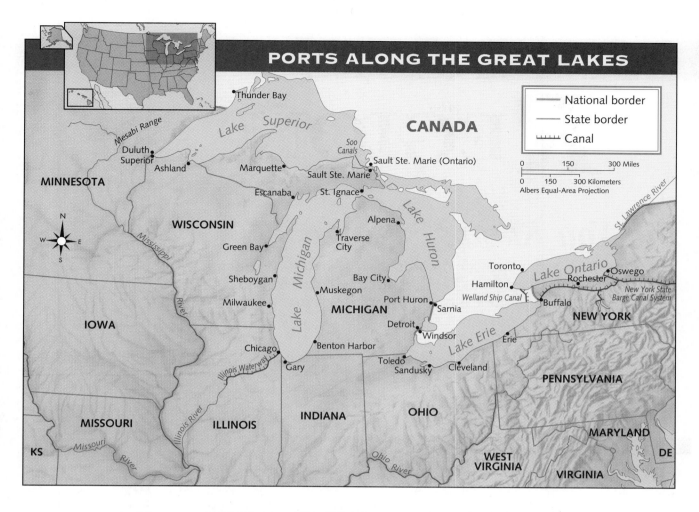

PORTS ALONG THE GREAT LAKES

Thunder Bay

Lake Superior

CANADA

Mesabi Range

Soo Canals

Duluth
Superior
Ashland

Sault Ste. Marie (Ontario)

MINNESOTA

Marquette

Sault Ste. Marie

Escanaba

St. Ignace

Alpena

WISCONSIN

Traverse City

Lake Huron

Green Bay

Lake Michigan

Toronto

Lake Ontario
Rochester
Oswego

Hamilton

New York State
Barge Canal System

Sheboygan

Bay City

Muskegon

Welland Ship Canal

Buffalo

IOWA

Milwaukee

MICHIGAN

Port Huron

Sarnia

NEW YORK

Detroit

Chicago

Benton Harbor

Windsor

Lake Erie

Erie

Illinois Waterway

Gary

Toledo

Cleveland

PENNSYLVANIA

KS

Missouri River

Illinois River

ILLINOIS

Sandusky

INDIANA

OHIO

MARYLAND

MISSOURI

Ohio River

WEST
VIRGINIA

VIRGINIA

DE

St. Lawrence River

Mississippi River

Legend:
- National border
- State border
- Canal

0   150   300 Miles
0   150   300 Kilometers
Albers Equal-Area Projection

N
W — E
S

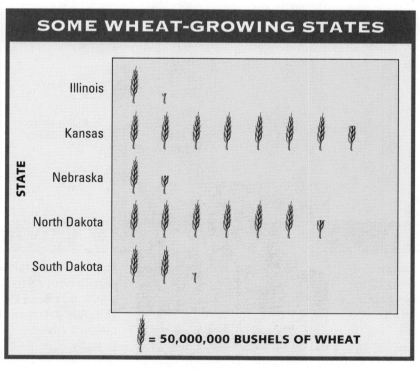

SOME WHEAT-GROWING STATES

STATE

Illinois

Kansas

Nebraska

North Dakota

South Dakota

= 50,000,000 BUSHELS OF WHEAT

REGION

Did You Know?

The Southwest region is made up of four large states—Arizona, New Mexico, Oklahoma, and Texas. It stretches west from the Gulf Coast of Texas to the Colorado River in Arizona. Mexico borders the region on the south.

STATE	CAPITAL	NICKNAME	POPULATION*	TEN LARGEST CITIES	LEADING PRODUCTS AND RESOURCES

THE SOUTHWEST STATES

STATE	CAPITAL	NICKNAME	POPULATION*
Arizona (AZ)	Phoenix	Grand Canyon State	4,554,000
New Mexico (NM)	Santa Fe	Land of Enchantment	1,729,000
Oklahoma (OK)	Oklahoma City	Sooner State	3,317,000
Texas (TX)	Austin	Lone Star State	19,439,000

*The most recent figures available.

TEN LARGEST CITIES
1. Houston, Texas
2. Dallas, Texas
3. Phoenix, Arizona
4. San Antonio, Texas
5. El Paso, Texas
6. Austin, Texas
7. Fort Worth, Texas
8. Oklahoma City, Oklahoma
9. Tucson, Arizona
10. Albuquerque, New Mexico

Farming:
Beef cattle, citrus fruits, cotton, dairy cows, grain sorghum, hay, melons, rice, sheep, vegetables, wheat
Fishing:
Crabs, fish, oysters, shrimp
Manufacturing:
Chemicals, dairy products, electrical equipment, machinery, metal products, petroleum products, processed foods
Mining:
Coal, copper, natural gas, oil, potash, silver,

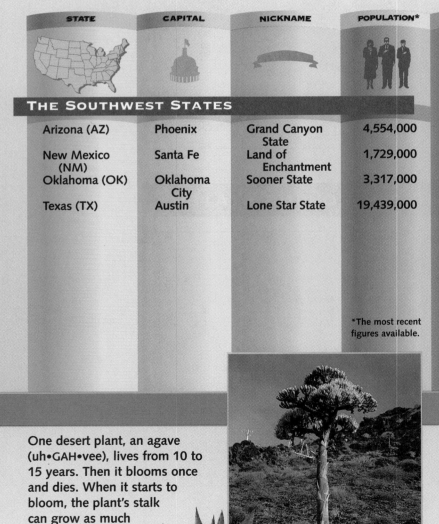

One desert plant, an agave (uh•GAH•vee), lives from 10 to 15 years. Then it blooms once and dies. When it starts to bloom, the plant's stalk can grow as much as 16 inches (41 cm) in 24 hours.

There are more telescopes near Tucson, Arizona, than anywhere else in the world. The clear desert air there makes it easier to study the stars.

THE SOUTHWEST

Legend:
- ★ State capital
- National park
- ▲ Mountain peak

WY

NE

NV

UT

CO

GREAT

KS

MO

ROCKY MOUNTAINS

Arkansas River

Colorado River

Lake Powell

Colorado

Grand Canyon National Park

Plateau

Four Corners

Painted Desert

▲ Wheeler Peak 13,161 ft. (4,011 m)

Guymon

CENTRAL PLAINS

OKLAHOMA

Arkansas River

Tulsa

Lake Mead

Hoover Dam

Bullhead City

Flagstaff

Gallup

★ Santa Fe

Albuquerque

Amarillo

Canadian River

Elk City

★ Oklahoma City

Lawton

AR

Ouachita Mountains

CA

ARIZONA

Petrified Forest National Park

NEW MEXICO

Clovis

Red River

Wichita Falls

Lake Texoma

Colorado River

Sun City

Phoenix

★ Mesa

Salt River

Rio Grande

Roswell

Lubbock

Fort Worth

Sabine River

Dallas

LA

Casa Grande

Gila River

Carlsbad Caverns National Park

Midland

Abilene

TEXAS

Yuma

Sonoran Desert

Tucson

Las Cruces

Chihuahuan Desert

El Paso

Guadalupe Mountains National Park

Pecos River

Odessa

San Angelo

Colorado River

Brazos River

Trinity River

Beaumont

Houston

Big Bend National Park

★ Austin

Galveston

Gulf of California

MEXICO

N W E S

San Antonio

COASTAL PLAIN

Laredo

Rio Grande

Corpus Christi

PACIFIC OCEAN

Brownsville

Gulf of Mexico

Scale:
0   100   200 Miles
0   100   200 Kilometers
Albers Equal-Area Projection

FIRE DANGER

EXTREME

TODAY!

PREVENT FOREST FIRES
DEPT. OF ENVIRONMENTAL RESOURCES

There was a real Smokey Bear. He was a brown bear cub rescued from a forest fire in New Mexico's Lincoln National Forest. Today a state park in New Mexico is named for him.

The Four Corners is the only place in the United States where four states meet at a single point. The states are Arizona, Colorado, New Mexico, and Utah.

79

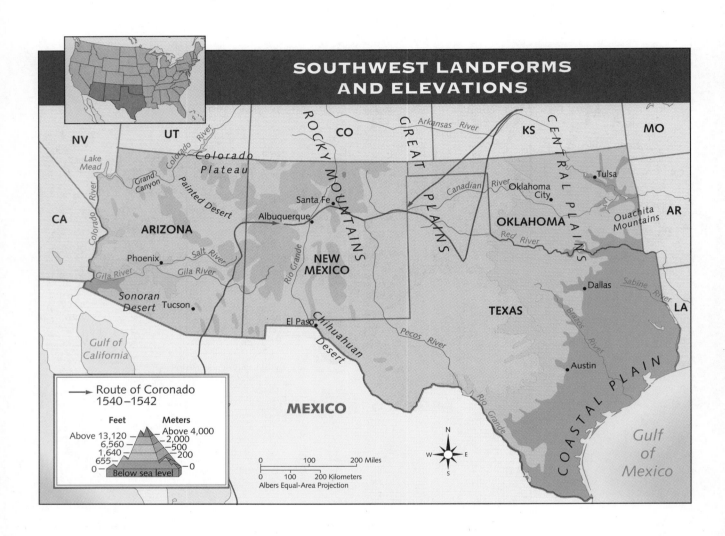

SOUTHWEST LANDFORMS AND ELEVATIONS

NV
UT
CO
KS
MO

Colorado River
Colorado Plateau
ROCKY MOUNTAINS
Arkansas River
GREAT PLAINS
CENTRAL PLAINS

Lake Mead
Grand Canyon
Painted Desert
Santa Fe
Canadian River
Oklahoma City
Tulsa

CA
Colorado River
ARIZONA
Albuquerque
NEW MEXICO
OKLAHOMA
Ouachita Mountains
AR

Phoenix
Salt River
Rio Grande
Red River

Gila River
Gila River
Dallas
Sabine River
LA

Sonoran Desert
Tucson
El Paso
TEXAS
Brazos River

Gulf of California
Chihuahuan Desert
Pecos River

MEXICO
Austin
COASTAL PLAIN

Rio Grande
Gulf of Mexico

→ Route of Coronado
1540–1542

Feet	Meters
Above 13,120	Above 4,000
6,560	2,000
1,640	500
655	200
0	0
Below sea level	

0   100   200 Miles
0   100   200 Kilometers
Albers Equal-Area Projection

N
W   E
S

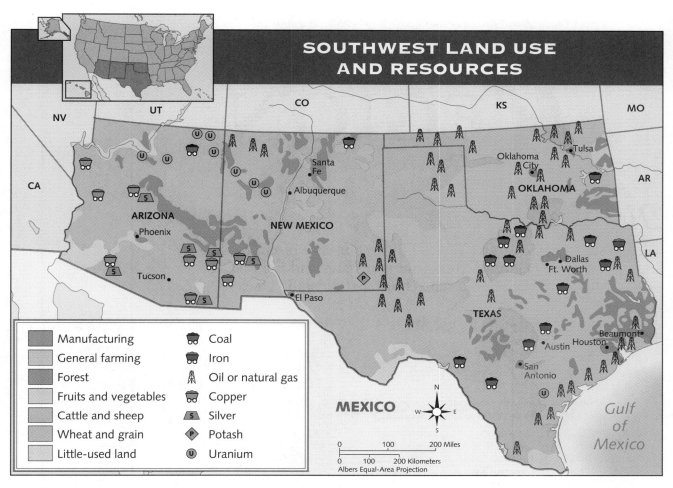

SOUTHWEST LAND USE AND RESOURCES

NV
UT
CO
KS
MO
CA
ARIZONA
Phoenix
Santa Fe
Albuquerque
NEW MEXICO
Oklahoma City
Tulsa
OKLAHOMA
AR
Tucson
El Paso
P
Dallas
Ft. Worth
LA
TEXAS
Beaumont
Austin
Houston
San Antonio

MEXICO

Gulf of Mexico

	Manufacturing		Coal
	General farming		Iron
	Forest		Oil or natural gas
	Fruits and vegetables		Copper
	Cattle and sheep	S	Silver
	Wheat and grain	P	Potash
	Little-used land	U	Uranium

N W E S

0   100   200 Miles
0 100 200 Kilometers
Albers Equal-Area Projection

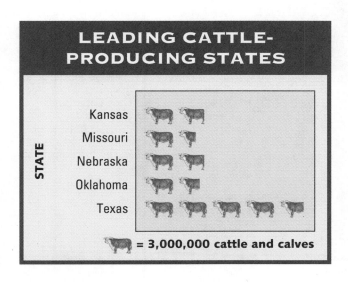

LEADING CATTLE-PRODUCING STATES

STATE

Kansas
Missouri
Nebraska
Oklahoma
Texas

= 3,000,000 cattle and calves

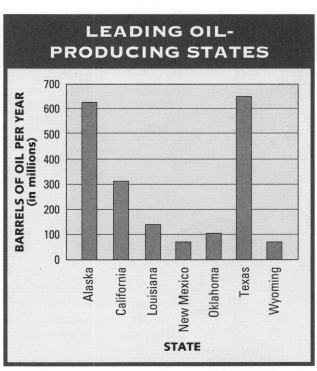

LEADING OIL-PRODUCING STATES

BARRELS OF OIL PER YEAR (in millions)

700
600
500
400
300
200
100
0

Alaska
California
Louisiana
New Mexico
Oklahoma
Texas
Wyoming

STATE

REGION

Did You Know?

Eleven states make up the West. Those states are often divided into two smaller regions—the Mountain states and the Pacific states. All five of the Pacific states border the Pacific Ocean.

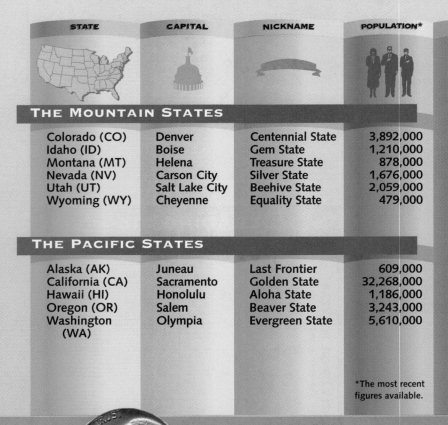

STATE	CAPITAL	NICKNAME	POPULATION*	TEN LARGEST CITIES	LEADING PRODUCTS AND RESOURCES
THE MOUNTAIN STATES				1. Los Angeles, California	**Farming:** Barley, beef cattle, coffee, cotton, dairy cows, fruits, hay, potatoes, rice, sheep, sugar beets, sugarcane, vegetables, wheat
Colorado (CO)	Denver	Centennial State	3,892,000	2. San Diego, California	
Idaho (ID)	Boise	Gem State	1,210,000	3. San Jose, California	
Montana (MT)	Helena	Treasure State	878,000	4. San Francisco, California	
Nevada (NV)	Carson City	Silver State	1,676,000	5. Seattle, Washington	**Fishing:** Crabs, fish, oysters, scallops, shrimp
Utah (UT)	Salt Lake City	Beehive State	2,059,000	6. Denver, Colorado	**Manufacturing:** Chemicals, dairy products, electrical equipment, jet airplanes, lumber, metal products, paper products, processed foods, machinery
Wyoming (WY)	Cheyenne	Equality State	479,000	7. Portland, Oregon	
THE PACIFIC STATES				8. Long Beach, California	
Alaska (AK)	Juneau	Last Frontier	609,000	9. Sacramento, California	
California (CA)	Sacramento	Golden State	32,268,000	10. Fresno, California	
Hawaii (HI)	Honolulu	Aloha State	1,186,000		**Mining:** Coal, copper, gold, lead, natural gas, oil, silver, uranium, zinc
Oregon (OR)	Salem	Beaver State	3,243,000		
Washington (WA)	Olympia	Evergreen State	5,610,000		

*The most recent figures available.

The U.S. Mint in Denver, Colorado, can make as many as 40 million coins a day. It makes many of the coins used throughout the United States.

Crater Lake, in Oregon, is the deepest lake in the United States. In one place it is 1,932 feet (589 m) deep.

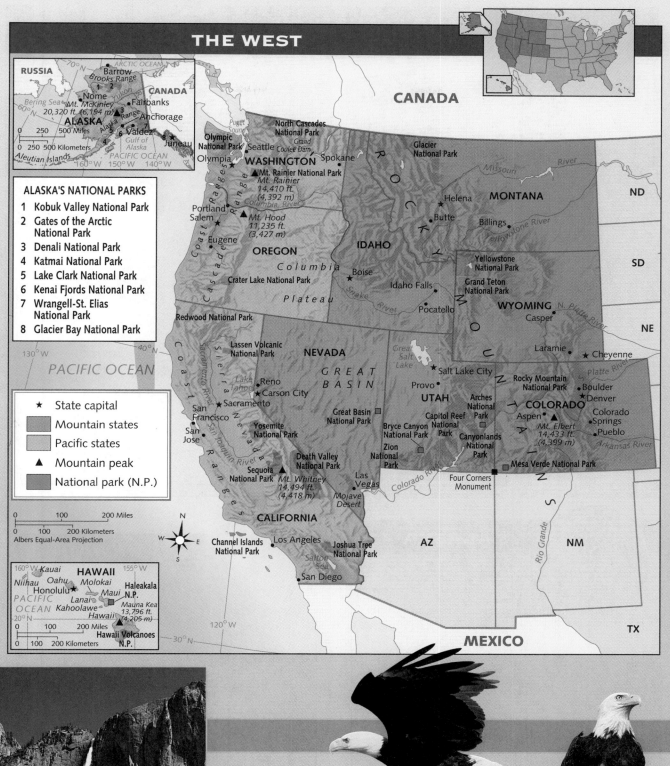

THE WEST

ALASKA'S NATIONAL PARKS

1 Kobuk Valley National Park
2 Gates of the Arctic National Park
3 Denali National Park
4 Katmai National Park
5 Lake Clark National Park
6 Kenai Fjords National Park
7 Wrangell-St. Elias National Park
8 Glacier Bay National Park

Legend

★ State capital
Mountain states
Pacific states
▲ Mountain peak
National park (N.P.)

0 — 100 — 200 Miles
0 — 100 — 200 Kilometers
Albers Equal-Area Projection

Alaska inset:
RUSSIA
Barrow
Brooks Range
Nome
Mt. McKinley 20,320 ft. (6,194 m)
ALASKA
Fairbanks
Anchorage
Valdez
Juneau
CANADA
ARCTIC OCEAN
Bering Sea
Gulf of Alaska
PACIFIC OCEAN
Aleutian Islands
Alaska Range
Yukon
0 — 250 — 500 Miles
0 — 250 — 500 Kilometers
70° N   60° N
160° W   150° W   140° W

Hawaii inset:
HAWAII
Kauai
Niihau
Oahu
Honolulu
Molokai
Lanai
Maui
Haleakala N.P.
Kahoolawe
Hawaii
Mauna Kea 13,796 ft. (4,205 m)
Hawaii Volcanoes N.P.
PACIFIC OCEAN
160° W   155° W   20° N   30° N
0 — 100 — 200 Miles
0 — 100 — 200 Kilometers

Main map labels:
CANADA
MEXICO
PACIFIC OCEAN
130° W   120° W   40° N   30° N

WASHINGTON — Seattle, Olympia, Spokane
Olympic National Park, North Cascades National Park, Grand Coulee Dam, Puget Sound
Mt. Rainier National Park, Mt. Rainier 14,410 ft. (4,392 m)
OREGON — Portland, Salem, Eugene
Mt. Hood 11,235 ft. (3,427 m)
Crater Lake National Park
Columbia River, Columbia Plateau
Redwood National Park
Coast Ranges, Cascade Range

MONTANA — Helena, Butte, Billings
Glacier National Park
Missouri River, Yellowstone River

IDAHO — Boise, Idaho Falls, Pocatello
Snake River

WYOMING — Casper, Laramie, Cheyenne
Yellowstone National Park, Grand Teton National Park
N. Platte River, Platte River

NEVADA — Reno, Carson City
Lassen Volcanic National Park, Great Basin National Park
GREAT BASIN
Lake Tahoe

CALIFORNIA — Sacramento, San Francisco, San Jose, Los Angeles, San Diego
Yosemite National Park, Sequoia National Park
Mt. Whitney 14,494 ft. (4,418 m)
Death Valley National Park
Channel Islands National Park, Joshua Tree National Park
Mojave Desert, Salton Sea
Sacramento River, San Joaquin River
Sierra Nevada

UTAH — Salt Lake City, Provo
Great Salt Lake
Arches National Park, Capitol Reef National Park, Bryce Canyon National Park, Zion National Park, Canyonlands National Park
Colorado River

COLORADO — Denver, Boulder, Aspen, Colorado Springs, Pueblo
Rocky Mountain National Park, Mesa Verde National Park
Mt. Elbert 14,433 ft. (4,399 m)
Arkansas River
Four Corners Monument

ROCKY MOUNTAINS
ND   SD   NE
AZ   NM   TX

Yosemite Falls, in California, is 13 times higher than Niagara Falls.

More bald eagles gather along the Chilkat River, in Alaska, than at any other place in the world. They fly there to catch salmon from the river.

LANDFORMS AND ELEVATIONS IN THE WEST

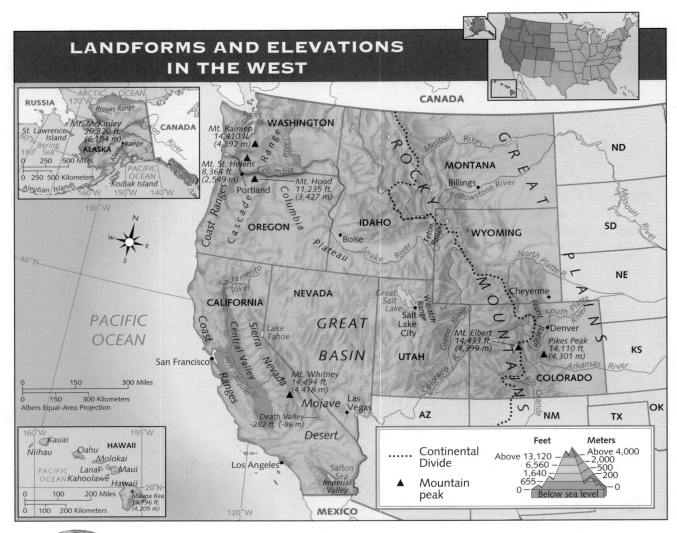

RUSSIA · ARCTIC OCEAN · 170°W · Brooks Range · CANADA
Mt. McKinley 20,320 ft. (6,194 m) · St. Lawrence Island · 60°N · Bering Sea · 180° · ALASKA · Alaska Range · Yukon River
PACIFIC OCEAN · Kodiak Island · Aleutian Islands · 160°W · 150°W · 140°W

0 250 500 Miles
0 250 500 Kilometers

CANADA

WASHINGTON
Mt. Rainier 14,410 ft. (4,392 m) ▲
Puget Sound
Mt. St. Helens 8,364 ft. (2,549 m) ▲
Columbia River
Portland
Mt. Hood 11,235 ft. (3,427 m)
Coast Ranges
Cascade Range
OREGON
Columbia Plateau
Sacramento River

ROCKY
Missouri River
GREAT
MONTANA
Billings
Yellowstone River
IDAHO
Boise
Snake River
Teton Range
WYOMING
North Platte R.
ND
Missouri River
SD
NE
Cheyenne
South Platte River
PLAINS

NEVADA
CALIFORNIA
Coast Ranges
Sierra Nevada
Central Valley
San Joaquin R.
Lake Tahoe
GREAT BASIN
Great Salt Lake
Wasatch Range
Salt Lake City
UTAH
Green River
Colorado R.
MOUNTAINS
Mt. Elbert 14,433 ft. (4,399 m) ▲
Front Range
Denver
Pikes Peak 14,110 ft. (4,301 m) ▲
Arkansas River
COLORADO
KS

130°W
40°N
PACIFIC OCEAN
San Francisco
Mt. Whitney 14,494 ft. (4,418 m) ▲
Mojave
Las Vegas
Death Valley -282 ft. (-86 m)
Los Angeles
Desert
Salton Sea
Imperial Valley
AZ
NM
Rio Grande
TX
OK

0 150 300 Miles
0 150 300 Kilometers
Albers Equal-Area Projection

160°W · 155°W
Kauai · Niihau · Oahu · **HAWAII** · Molokai · Lanai · Maui · Kahoolawe · Hawaii · 20°N
PACIFIC OCEAN
Mauna Kea 13,796 ft. (4,205 m)
0 100 200 Miles
0 100 200 Kilometers

120°W
MEXICO

Feet	Meters
..... Continental Divide	Above 13,120 — Above 4,000
	6,560 — 2,000
	1,640 — 500
	655 — 200
▲ Mountain peak	0 — 0
	Below sea level

ALASKA

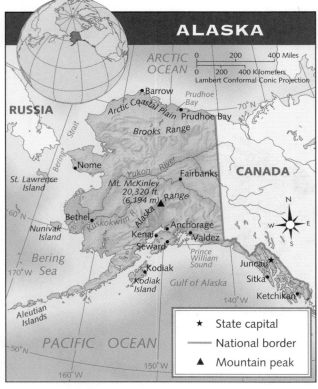

ARCTIC OCEAN
0 200 400 Miles
0 200 400 Kilometers
Lambert Conformal Conic Projection

Barrow
Prudhoe Bay
Arctic Coastal Plain
Prudhoe Bay
70°N
Brooks Range
RUSSIA
Bering Strait
Nome
Yukon River
Fairbanks
CANADA
St. Lawrence Island
Mt. McKinley 20,320 ft. (6,194 m) ▲
Alaska Range
60°N
Bethel
Kuskokwim R.
Anchorage
Nunivak Island
Kenai
Valdez
Seward
Prince William Sound
Juneau ★
Bering Sea
Kodiak
170°W
Kodiak Island
Gulf of Alaska
Sitka
140°W
Ketchikan
Aleutian Islands
50°N
150°W
160°W
PACIFIC OCEAN

★ State capital
— National border
▲ Mountain peak

HAWAII

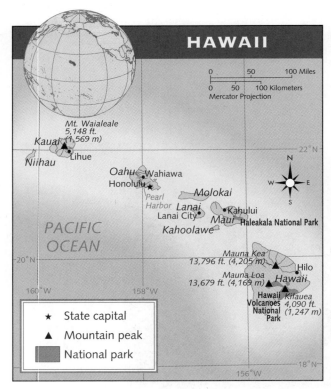

0 50 100 Miles
0 50 100 Kilometers
Mercator Projection

Mt. Waialeale 5,148 ft. (1,569 m) ▲
Kauai
Lihue
Niihau
22°N
Oahu
Wahiawa
Honolulu
Pearl Harbor
Molokai
Lanai
Lanai City
Maui
Kahului
Haleakala National Park
Kahoolawe
PACIFIC OCEAN
20°N
Mauna Kea 13,796 ft. (4,205 m) ▲
Mauna Loa 13,679 ft. (4,169 m) ▲
Hilo
Hawaii
Hawaii Volcanoes National Park
Kilauea 4,090 ft. (1,247 m)
160°W
158°W
156°W
18°N

★ State capital
▲ Mountain peak
■ National park

THE PACIFIC NORTHWEST

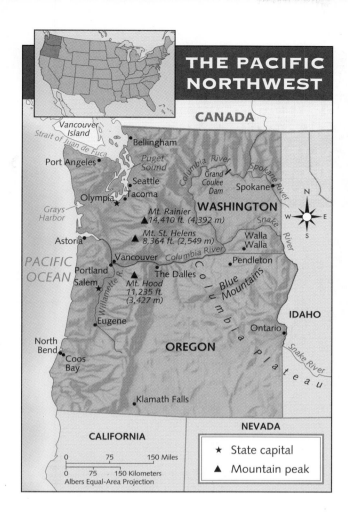

CANADA

Vancouver Island
Strait of Juan de Fuca
Bellingham
Port Angeles
Puget Sound
Seattle
Tacoma
Olympia
Grays Harbor
WASHINGTON
Mt. Rainier ▲ 14,410 ft. (4,392 m)
Mt. St. Helens ▲ 8,364 ft. (2,549 m)
Walla Walla
Spokane
Spokane River
Grand Coulee Dam
Columbia River
Snake River
Astoria
Vancouver
Columbia River
Pendleton
PACIFIC OCEAN
Portland
Salem
Mt. Hood ▲ 11,235 ft. (3,427 m)
The Dalles
Columbia Plateau
Blue Mountains
IDAHO
Willamette R.
Eugene
Ontario
Snake River
North Bend
Coos Bay
OREGON
Klamath Falls
CALIFORNIA
NEVADA

| 0 | 75 | 150 Miles |
| 0 | 75 | 150 Kilometers |

Albers Equal-Area Projection

★ State capital
▲ Mountain peak

GUAM

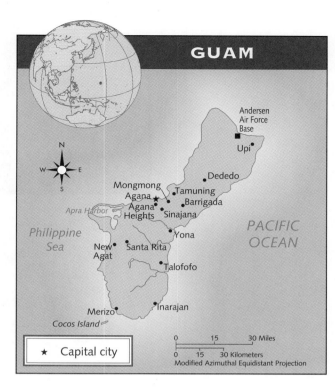

Andersen Air Force Base
Upi
N W E S
Mongmong
Agana
Dededo
Tamuning
Barrigada
Agana Heights
Sinajana
Apra Harbor
Philippine Sea
Yona
New Agat
Santa Rita
Talofofo
PACIFIC OCEAN
Merizo
Inarajan
Cocos Island

★ Capital city

| 0 | 15 | 30 Miles |
| 0 | 15 | 30 Kilometers |

Modified Azimuthal Equidistant Projection

AVERAGE HEIGHT OF THREE KINDS OF TREES

White oak
60–80 feet
(18–24 m)

Giant sequoia
250 feet
(76 m)

Redwood
300 feet
(91m)

INSIDE A VOLCANO

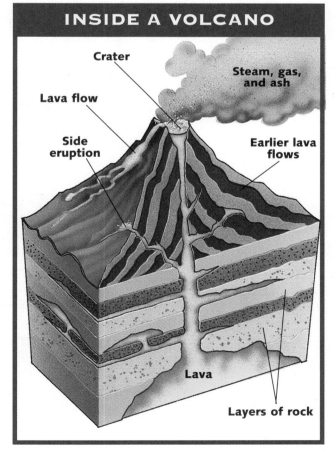

Crater
Steam, gas, and ash
Lava flow
Side eruption
Earlier lava flows
Lava
Layers of rock

85

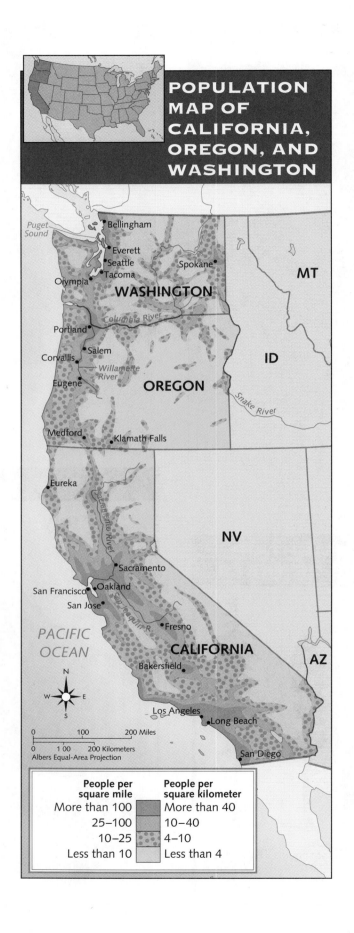

POPULATION MAP OF CALIFORNIA, OREGON, AND WASHINGTON

Puget Sound

Bellingham

Everett
Seattle
Tacoma
Olympia

Spokane

WASHINGTON

MT

Columbia River

Portland

Salem
Corvallis

ID

Willamette River

Eugene

OREGON

Snake River

Medford

Klamath Falls

Eureka

NV

Sacramento River

San Joaquin R.

Sacramento

San Francisco
Oakland
San Jose

Fresno

PACIFIC OCEAN

CALIFORNIA

AZ

Bakersfield

N
W   E
S

Los Angeles
Long Beach

0   100   200 Miles

0   1 00   200 Kilometers
Albers Equal-Area Projection

San Diego

People per square mile	People per square kilometer
More than 100	More than 40
25–100	10–40
10–25	4–10
Less than 10	Less than 4

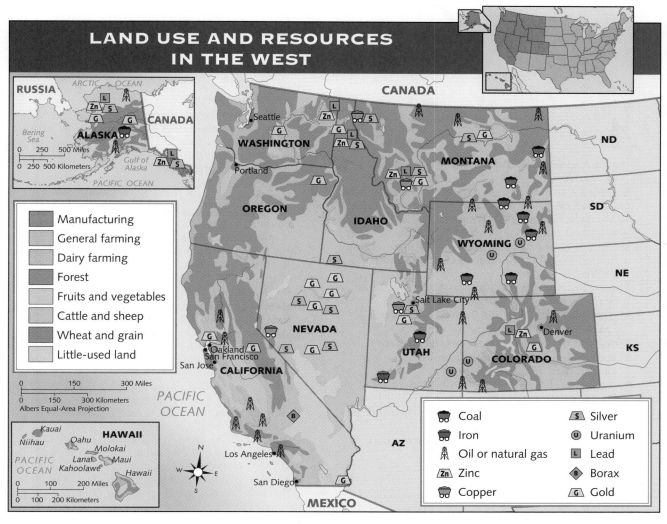

LAND USE AND RESOURCES IN THE WEST

RUSSIA

ARCTIC OCEAN

CANADA

Bering Sea

ALASKA

0 250 500 Miles
0 250 500 Kilometers

Gulf of Alaska

PACIFIC OCEAN

Legend:
- Manufacturing
- General farming
- Dairy farming
- Forest
- Fruits and vegetables
- Cattle and sheep
- Wheat and grain
- Little-used land

0 150 300 Miles
0 150 300 Kilometers
Albers Equal-Area Projection

HAWAII
Kauai
Niihau
Oahu
Molokai
Lanai Maui
Kahoolawe
Hawaii

PACIFIC OCEAN

0 100 200 Miles
0 100 200 Kilometers

CANADA

Seattle

WASHINGTON

Portland

OREGON

IDAHO

MONTANA

WYOMING

ND

SD

NE

Salt Lake City

UTAH

Denver

COLORADO

KS

NEVADA

Oakland
San Francisco
San Jose

CALIFORNIA

PACIFIC OCEAN

Los Angeles

San Diego

N W E S

AZ

MEXICO

Resources legend:
- Coal
- Iron
- Oil or natural gas
- Zinc (Zn)
- Copper
- Silver (S)
- Uranium (U)
- Lead (L)
- Borax (B)
- Gold (G)

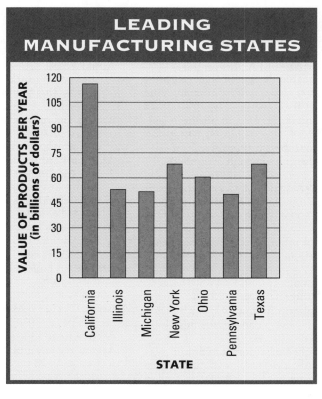

LEADING MANUFACTURING STATES

VALUE OF PRODUCTS PER YEAR
(in billions of dollars)

120
105
90
75
60
45
30
15
0

California
Illinois
Michigan
New York
Ohio
Pennsylvania
Texas

STATE

GAZETTEER

The Gazetteer is a geographical dictionary that will help you locate places.
The page number tells where each place appears on a map in this atlas.

A

Acadia National Park A national park on the coast of Maine. p. 67

Acapulco A seaport in Guerrero state, Mexico, on the Pacific Ocean. (17°N, 100°W) p. 31

Adirondack Mountains (a•duh•RAHN•dak) A mountain range in northeastern New York. p. 67

Adriatic Sea An extension of the Mediterranean Sea; located east of Italy and west of the Balkan Peninsula. p. 26

Aegean Sea (ih•JEE•uhn) An arm of the Mediterranean Sea between Asia Minor and Greece. p. 26

Afghanistan A country in Asia; located between Pakistan and Iran. p. 24

Africa One of the world's seven continents. p. 19

Al Basrah A port city in southeastern Iraq, near the Persian Gulf. (31°N, 48°E) p. 24

Alabama River A river in the southeastern United States. p. 71

Alaska Range A mountain range in southern Alaska. p. 84

Albania A European country located on the Balkan Peninsula on the Adriatic Sea. p. 19

Albany (AWL•ban•ee) The capital of New York. (43°N, 74°W) p. 67

Alberta One of Canada's ten provinces. p. 30

Albuquerque (AL•buh•ker•kee) The largest city in New Mexico. (35°N, 107°W) p. 79

Aleutian Islands (uh•LOO•shuhn) A chain of volcanic islands extending southwest from the Alaska Peninsula; they separate the Bering Sea from the Pacific Ocean. (52°N, 175°W) p. 84

Alexandria (a•lig•ZAN•dree•uh) A port on the Mediterranean Sea; located on the northern coast of Egypt on the Nile delta; also the name of many cities founded by Alexander the Great. (31°N, 30°E) p. 22

Algiers The capital of Algeria; located in northern central Algeria on the Bay of Algiers. (36°N, 2°E) p. 22

Allegheny Mountains (a•luh•GAY•nee) A mountain range that is part of the Appalachian Mountains. p. 67

Allegheny River (a•luh•GAY•nee) A river in the northeastern United States, joining the Monongahela River at Pittsburgh, Pennsylvania, to form the Ohio River. p. 67

Alps The largest group of mountains in Europe; located in France, Switzerland, Italy, Austria, Slovenia, and Croatia. p. 26

Altai Mountains A mountain system in Asia where Russia, China, and Mongolia meet. p. 27

Altamaha River (AWL•tuh•muh•haw) A river that begins in southeastern Georgia and flows into the Atlantic Ocean. p. 71

Amazon Basin An area of tropical forest in South America, located mainly in Brazil. p. 29

Amazon River The longest river in South America, flowing from the Andes Mountains, across Brazil, and into the Atlantic Ocean. p. 29

American Samoa (suh•MOH•uh) A United States territory in the Pacific Ocean. p. 18

Amman The capital of Jordan, located northeast of the Dead Sea. (32°N, 36°E) p. 24

Amsterdam The capital and largest city of the Netherlands; located on the IJ River in the western central Netherlands. (52°N, 5°E) p. 24

Amur River A river in northeastern Asia; forms part of the border between Russia and China. p. 27

Anchorage (ANG•kuh•rihj) The largest city in Alaska. (61°N, 150°W) p. 84

Andaman Sea A body of water southeast of Asia; forms the eastern part of the Bay of Bengal. p. 27

Andes Mountains (AN•deez) The mountains extending along the west coast of South America from Panama to Tierra del Fuego; the longest chain of mountains in the world. p. 29

Angola A former part of the historic African kingdom of Kongo and a colony of Portugal; present-day country in southern Africa on the Atlantic coast. (12°S, 18°E) p. 22

Annapolis (uh•NAH•puh•luhs) The capital of Maryland; located on Chesapeake Bay; home of the United States Naval Academy. (39°N, 76°W) p. 67

Antarctic Circle (ant•AHRK•tihk) The line of latitude that is located at 66½°S. p. 21

Antarctica One of the world's seven continents. p. 21

Antigua and Barbuda An island nation in the eastern part of the Leeward Islands. p. 32

Apennine Mountains (AP•uh•nyn) A mountain range; runs north and south through the center of Italy. p. 26

Appalachian Mountains (a•puh•LAY•chuhn) A large chain of mountains that extends in the United States from Maine to northern Georgia and central Alabama. p. 51

Arabia The historic name for the lands now known as the Arabian Peninsula, the Sinai Peninsula, Syria, and Mesopotamia. p. 26

Arabian Peninsula A peninsula bordered by the Red Sea, the Persian Gulf, and the Arabian Sea in Southwest Asia; location of the present-day countries of Saudi Arabia, Yemen, Oman, the United Arab Emirates, Qatar, and Kuwait. p. 26

Arabian Sea The sea located west of India and east of the Arabian Peninsula; forms the southern border of Southwest Asia. p. 26

Aral Sea A large inland body of water, flowing through the countries of Kazakhstan and Uzbekistan in central Asia. p. 26

Arctic Circle (AHRK•tik) The line of latitude located at 66½°N. p. 20

Arctic Ocean One of the four oceans of the world. p. 20

Argentina A South American country on the Atlantic Coast. p. 28

Arkansas River A tributary of the Mississippi River, beginning in central Colorado and ending in Desha County, Arkansas. p. 71

Arkhangel'sk A Russian port city in Europe. (65°N, 41°E) p. 24

Armenia An ancient kindgom in central Asia; a present-day country in Asia. p. 24

Asia One of the world's seven continents. p. 19

Asunción A city in South America, located on the eastern bank of the Paraguay River where the Paraguay and Pilcomayo rivers join. (25°S, 57°W) p. 28

Aswan Ancient trade center; present-day city located on the Nile River near Lake Nasser in southeastern Egypt; near the site of the Aswan Dam. (24°N, 33°E) p. 22

Atacama Desert (a•tah•KAH•mah) A desert region in South America; the driest desert in the world. p. 29

Athabasca River A south tributary of the Mackenzie River in Alberta, western central Canada; flows northeast and then north into Lake Athabasca. p. 29

Athens A city-state of ancient Greece; capital of present-day Greece; located near the southeastern coast of Greece. (38°N, 24°E) p. 24

Atlanta Georgia's capital and largest city. (33°N, 84°W) p. 71

Atlantic Ocean One of the world's four oceans. p. 20

Atlas Mountains A mountain system in North Africa. p. 23

Augusta A city located in eastern Georgia on the Savannah River. (33°N, 82°W) p. 58

Augusta The capital of Maine. (44°N, 70°W) p. 67

Austin The capital of Texas. (30°N, 98°W) p. 79

Australia One of the world's seven continents; a present-day country filling the continent of Australia. (23°S, 135°E) p. 19

Austria A country in central Europe. p. 19

Azerbaijan (a•zer•by•JAHN) A country in southeastern Europe; located west of the Caspian Sea; formerly part of the Soviet Union. p. 24

B

Baffin Bay A large inlet of the Atlantic Ocean between western Greenland and eastern Baffin Island; connects with the Atlantic Ocean by the Davis Strait. p. 29

Baffin Island Land partially in the Arctic Circle west of Greenland. p. 29

Baghdad The capital of Iraq; located on both sides of the Tigris River in the eastern part of the country. (33°N, 44°E) p. 24

Bahama Islands Independent state comprising a chain of islands, cays, and reefs lying southeast of Florida and north of Cuba. p. 28

Baja Peninsula A peninsula extending south southeast between the Pacific Ocean and the Gulf of California, in northwestern Mexico. p. 29

Balearic Islands (bal•ee•AIR•ik) An island group in the western Mediterranean Sea, off the eastern coast of Spain; forms the Spanish province of Baleares. (39°N, 3°E) p. 26

Balkan Peninsula A peninsula extending from mainland Europe into the Mediterranean Sea; occupied by Greece, Albania, Slovenia, Croatia, Bosnia and Herzegovina, Serbia, Montenegro, Romania, Bulgaria, and Turkey. p. 26

Baltic Sea The sea located on the southern side of the Scandinavian Peninsula. p. 26

Baltimore A major seaport in Maryland; located on the Patapsco River at Chesapeake Bay. (39°N, 77°W) p. 67

Bangalore The capital city of Karnataka; located in southern India. p. 24

Bangkok The capital of Thailand; located on the southern end of the Chao Phraya River on the Gulf of Thailand. (14°N, 101°E) p. 25

Bangladesh (bahn•gluh•DESH) A country in South Asia on the coast of the Bay of Bengal. p. 25

Banks Island An island in western Franklin district, Northwest Territories, Canada. p. 29

Barbados An island in the Lesser Antilles, West Indies; located east of the central Windward Islands. p. 32

Barcelona A province and city of Spain; located northeast of Madrid. p. 24

Barents Sea A sea comprising the part of the Arctic Ocean between Spitsbergen and Novaya Zemlya. p. 26

Baton Rouge (BA•tuhn ROOZH) The capital of Louisiana. (30°N, 91°W) p. 71

Bay of Bengal An inlet of the Indian Ocean between India and the Indochina Peninsula. p. 27

Beaufort Sea A sea that is northeast of Alaska, northwest of Canada, and west of Banks Island in the Arctic Islands. p. 29

Beijing (BAY•JING) The capital of China; located in northeastern China; present-day name for Kublai Khan's historic capital of Khanbalik. (40°N, 116°E) p. 25

Belarus A country located north of Ukraine, west of Russia, and east of Poland; formerly part of the Soviet Union. p. 24

Belém A seaport city in northern Brazil, on the Pará River. (1°S, 48°W) p. 28

Belgium A country in Europe, on the coast of the North Sea. p. 19

Belgrade The capital of Serbia; located at the junction of the Sava and Danube rivers. (45°N, 21°E) p. 24

Belize (bay•LEEZ) A country in Central America, near the Caribbean Sea. p. 28

Belmopan A town in Central America; capital of Belize. (17°N, 88°W) p. 28

Belo Horizonte A city in eastern Brazil. (20°S, 44°W) p. 28

Benin (buh•NIN) A former kingdom of West Africa; present-day country in West Africa. (10°N, 12°W) p. 22

Bering Sea A sea separating Alaska and Russia. p. 27

Bering Strait A narrow water passage separating Asia from North America. p. 27

Berlin The capital of Germany; located in the northeastern part of Germany. (53°N, 13°E) p. 24

Bern The capital of Switzerland. (47°N, 7°E) p. 24

Bhutan (boo•TAN) A country in Asia, south of China and north of India. p. 25

Big Bend National Park A national park on the big bend of the Rio Grande, in western Texas. p. 79

Birmingham A city located northwest of London. (52°N, 2°W) p. 24

Birmingham A large city in Alabama; located near iron and coal deposits. (33°N, 86°W) p. 71

Biscayne National Park (bis•KAYN) A national park in southern Florida. p. 71

Bismarck The capital of North Dakota. (47°N, 101°W) p. 75

Black Hills A group of mountains in South Dakota; its highest peak, more than 7,000 feet (2,134 m), is the highest point in the Plains states. p. 51

Black Sea A sea between Europe and Asia; surrounded by Bulgaria, Romania, Moldova, Ukraine, Russia, Georgia, and Turkey. p. 26

Bogotá A city in South America located on the plateau of the Andes; capital of Colombia. (4°N, 74°W) p. 28

Boise (BOY•zee) Idaho's capital and largest city. (44°N, 116°W) p. 83

Bolivia A country in west-central South America. p. 28

Bombay A city on the western coast of central India, also known as Mumbai. (19°N, 73°E) p. 24

Borneo An island in the Malay Archipelago. (1°N, 115°E) p. 25

Bosnia and Herzegovina (BAHZ•nee•uh hairt•suh•goh•VEE•nuh) A country in Europe; part of the former Yugoslavia. p. 19

Boston The capital and largest city of Massachusetts; settled by the Puritans in 1630. (42°N, 71°W) p. 67

Boston Harbor The western section of Massachusetts Bay; located in eastern Massachusetts; the city of Boston is located at its western end. p. 68

Botswana A country in southern Africa. p. 22

Brahmaputra River A river in southern Asia; flows through China, India, and Bangladesh into the Bay of Bengal. p. 27

Brasília A city in South America on the Paraná River; capital of Brazil. (15°S, 48°W) p. 28

Brazil The largest and most populous country in South America; the fifth-largest nation in the world. p. 28

Brazos River (BRAH•zohs) A river in central Texas; formed by the junction of the Salt Fork and Double Mountain Fork rivers in northern Texas; flows southeast into the Gulf of Mexico. p. 79

British Columbia One of Canada's ten provinces; located on the west coast of Canada. p. 30

British Isles The islands of Ireland and Great Britain; located off the northwestern coast of mainland Europe. (54°N, 4°W) p. 26

Brooks Range A mountain range in northern Alaska. p. 84

Brunei A country in northeastern Borneo. (5°N, 115°E) p. 25

Brussels The capital city of Belgium in Europe. (51°N, 4°E) p. 24

Bucharest The capital city of Romania. (44°N, 26°E) p. 24

Budapest The capital city of Hungary; includes the former towns of Buda and Pest. (47°N, 19°E) p. 24

Buenos Aires (BWAY•nahs IRE•ees) The capital city of Argentina, South America, on the Río de la Plata. (34°S, 58°W) p. 28

Buffalo A city in western New York; located on the Niagara River at Lake Erie. (43°N, 79°W) p. 67

Bulgaria A country in southeastern Europe; located on the Balkan Peninsula along the Black Sea. p. 19

Burkina Faso A country in Western Africa. p. 22

Burma (Myanmar) A country on the Indochina peninsula in Southeast Asia. p. 25

Burundi A country in Central Africa. p. 22

Butte (BYOOT) A city in southwestern Montana; located on the plateau of the Rocky Mountains. (46°N, 112°W) p. 83

C

Cahokia (kuh•HOH•kee•uh) An ancient settlement of the Mound Builders of the Mississippian culture; located near present-day East St. Louis, Illinois. p. 39

Cairo The capital of Egypt; located in northeastern Egypt on the Nile River. (30°N, 31°E) p. 22

Calcutta A port in northeastern India, near the Bay of Bengal. (23°N, 88°E) p. 25

Calgary A city in southern Alberta, Canada; located on Bow River. (51°N, 114°W) p. 28

Calicut A city in southwestern India, on the coast of the Arabian Sea. (11°N, 76°E) p. 39

Cambodia A country in Southeast Asia. p. 25

Cameroon (ka•muh•ROON) A former French and British colony; now an independent country in west-central Africa. p. 22

Canada The country located to the north of the United States; Canada and the United States share the longest undefended border in the world. p. 28

Canary Islands An island group in the Atlantic Ocean, off the northwestern coast of Africa. (29°N, 16°W) p. 23

Cape Canaveral (kuh•NAV•ruhl) A cape on the Atlantic coast of Florida. (28°N, 81°W) p. 71

Cape Cod A cape in southeastern Massachusetts; located between Cape Cod Bay and the Atlantic Ocean; Pilgrims sailing on the *Mayflower* landed here. (42°N, 70°W) p. 67

Cape Fear A cape in southeastern North Carolina. (34°N, 78°W) p. 51

Cape Fear River A river in central and southeastern North Carolina; formed by the Deep and Haw rivers; flows southeast into the Atlantic Ocean at eastern Brunswick County. p. 51

Cape Hatteras (HA•tuh•ruhs) A cape on Hatteras Island southeast of Dare County, North Carolina. (35°N, 75°W) p. 51

Cape Horn A cape on the southern tip of South America, on Horn Island; named by Dutch explorers. p. 29

Cape of Good Hope The southernmost tip of Africa, on the Atlantic Ocean. (34°S, 18°E) p. 23

Cape Town A seaport city of Cape Province and the capital of the country of South Africa. (34°S, 18°E) p. 22

Cape Verde An island country in the Atlantic Ocean, located off the coast of West Africa. (17°N, 25°W) p. 18

Cape Verde Islands (VERD) Islands off the west coast of Africa. (16°N, 24°W) p. 20

Caracas (kah•RAH•kahs) The capital city of Venezuela, South America; located near the coast of the Caribbean Sea. (10°N, 67°W) p. 28

Caribbean Sea (kair•uh•BEE•uhn) A part of the Atlantic Ocean bounded by the Lesser Antilles and Central and South America. p. 29

Carlsbad Caverns National Park A national park near Carlsbad, New Mexico. p. 79

Carson City The capital of Nevada. (39°N, 120°W) p. 83

Cascade Range A mountain range in the western United States; extends north from California to Oregon and Washington; Mt. Rainier is its highest peak. p. 83

Caspian Sea A salt lake between Europe and Asia, east of the Black Sea. p. 26

Catskill Mountains A mountain range in southeastern New York. p. 67

Caucasus Mountains (KAW•kuh•suhs) A mountain range between the Black and Caspian seas; borders Russia, Georgia, and Azerbaijan. p. 26

Cayenne A city on the northwestern coast of Cayenne Island; capital of French Guiana. (5°N, 52°W) p. 28

Celebes (SEL•uh•beez) An Indonesian island; located in Southeast Asia in the Malay Archipelago. (2°S, 120°E) p. 27

Central African Republic A country in Central Africa. p. 22

Central Valley A large valley in central California. p. 84

Ceylon See Sri Lanka.

Chad A country in North Africa. p. 22

Chang Jiang (CHAHNG jee•AHNG) A river in East Asia; flows from the Plateau of Tibet in southwestern China to the East China Sea. p. 27

Chang'an An ancient capital of the Han and the Tang dynasties of China; now known as Xian, Sian; located in central China on the Wei River. (34°N, 109°E) p. 25

Charleston A city in South Carolina; a major port on the Atlantic Ocean; once called Charles Towne. (33°N, 80°W) p. 71

Charleston The capital city of West Virginia. (38°N, 82°W) p. 71

Charlotte The largest city in North Carolina. (35°N, 81°W) p. 71

Charlottetown The capital of Prince Edward Island, Canada. (46°N, 63°W). p. 30

Chattahoochee River (chat•uh•HOO•chee) A river that begins in northeastern Georgia; flows southwest and south along the Alabama–Georgia border into the Gulf of Mexico. p. 71

Chattanooga (cha•tuh•NOO•guh) An industrial city on the Tennessee River in southeastern Tennessee. (35°N, 85°W) p. 71

Chennai A city formerly known as Madras. The capital of Tamil Nadu state, India (13°N, 80°E) p. 24

Cherokee Nation (CHAIR•uh•kee) An American Indian nation located in present-day northern Georgia, eastern Alabama, southern Tennessee, and western North Carolina. p. 57

Chesapeake Bay (CHEH•suh•peek) A bay on the Atlantic coast of the United States; it has its lower section in Virginia and its upper section in Maryland. p. 67

Cheyenne (shy•AN) The capital of Wyoming. (41°N, 105°W) p. 83

Chicago A city in Illinois; the third-largest city in the United States. (42°N, 88°W) p. 75

Chihuahua (chee•WAH•wah) A city and a state of northern Mexico. (29°N, 106°W) p. 31

Chihuahuan Desert (chee•WAH•wahn) A desert region that covers part of Mexico, New Mexico, and Texas; part of the North American Desert. p. 79

Chile A country on the southwestern coast of South America. p. 28

China A country in East Asia; it has the world's largest population. p. 25

Churchill River A river located in central Canada; flows east across Saskatchewan and north through Manitoba and then northeast into Hudson Bay. p. 30

Cincinnati (sin•suh•NA•tee) A city in southern Ohio. (39°N, 84°W) p. 75

Ciudad Juárez A city in northern Mexico, near El Paso. (31°N, 106°W) p. 31

Cleveland The largest city in Ohio; located at the mouth of the Cuyahoga River on Lake Erie. (41°N, 82°W) p. 75

Coast Ranges The mountain ranges that stretch along the Pacific coast of North America. p. 83

Coastal Plain One of two major plains in the United States; located along the coasts of the Atlantic Ocean and the Gulf of Mexico. p. 71

Colombia A country in northwestern South America. p. 28

Colorado Plateau A plateau in the southwestern United States; covers most of northern New Mexico and Arizona. p. 50

Colorado River A river in the southwestern United States; its basin extends from the Rocky Mountains to the Sierra Nevada; flows into the Gulf of California. p. 50

Columbia The capital of South Carolina. (34°N, 81°W) p. 71

Columbia Plateau A plateau located to the east of the Cascade Range. p. 50

Columbia River A river that begins in the Rocky Mountains in Canada, forms the Washington–Oregon border, and supplies much of that area's water-power. p. 83

Columbus The capital of Ohio. (40°N, 83°W) p. 75

Concord The capital of New Hampshire. (43°N, 72°W) p. 67

Congo, Democratic Republic of A country in Central Africa, formerly known as Zaire. p. 22

Congo, Republic of A country in Central Africa, east of Gabon. p. 22

Congo River A river located in southern Africa; begins in the central part of Zaire and flows into the Atlantic Ocean. p. 23

Connecticut River The longest river in New England; begins in New Hampshire, flows south through Massachusetts and Connecticut, and empties into Long Island Sound. p. 67

Constantinople (Istanbul) (kahn•stan•tuhn•OH•puhl) Formerly the ancient city of Byzantium; rebuilt, renamed, and made capital of the Byzantine Empire by Constantine I in 330; now known as Istanbul, Turkey. (41°N, 29°E) p. 39

Copenhagen The capital city and a port of Denmark. (56°N, 13°E) p. 24

Coral Sea A sea located north of Queensland, Australia, and south of Papua New Guinea. p. 34

Corpus Christi (KOHR•puhs KRIS•tee) A city in southern Texas. (28°N, 97°W) p. 79

Corsica A French island in the Mediterranean Sea, near the western coast of Italy. (42°N, 9°E) p. 26

Costa Rica A Central American country; located west of Panama, bordered by the Caribbean Sea and Pacific Ocean. (10°N, 84°W) p. 28

Côte d'Ivoire (koht dee•VWAHR) A country in West Africa; also known as the Ivory Coast. p. 22

Cozumel (koh•zooh•MEL) An island in the Caribbean Sea; located east of the Yucatán Peninsula; part of Mexico. p. 31

Crete A large Greek island; located southeast of the Balkan Peninsula; separates the Mediterranean and Aegean seas. (35°N, 25°E) p. 26

Croatia A country in southeastern Europe; part of the former Yugoslavia. p. 19

Cuba An island country in the Caribbean; the largest and westernmost island of the Caribbean Islands. (22°N, 79°W) p. 28

Cuernavaca A town in southern central Mexico. (19°N, 99°W) p. 31

Cumberland Gap A pass through the Appalachian Mountains; located in Tennessee; Daniel Boone traveled through this gap into Kentucky. p. 71

Cumberland River A river in southern Kentucky and northern Tennessee. p. 71

Cuzco (KOO•skoh) The capital of the ancient Inca Empire and a present-day city in southern Peru. (14°S, 72°W) p. 39

Cyprus An island country in the eastern Mediterranean Sea. (35°N, 33°E) p. 24

Czech Republic A country in central Europe; formerly part of Czechoslovakia. p. 19

D

Dallas An industrial city in northeastern Texas; located on the Trinity River. (38°N, 97°W) p. 79

Damascus The capital of Syria in Southwest Asia. (34°N, 36°E) p. 24

Danube River A river in central Europe; flows from southwest Germany to the Black Sea. p. 26

Davis Strait A strait between southwestern Greenland and eastern Baffin Island; connects Baffin Bay with the Atlantic Ocean. p. 29

Dawson A city in the Yukon Territory, Canada. (64°N, 139°W) p. 30

Dead Sea A salt lake in Israel and Jordan; the lowest place in the world, at 1,319 feet (402 m) below sea level. p. 26

Death Valley The lowest point in the Western Hemisphere; located in the Mojave Desert in California. (36°N, 117°W) p. 84

Deccan Plateau A triangle-shaped plateau in central India between the Western and Eastern Ghats. p. 26

Delaware Bay A bay on the coast of the Atlantic Ocean, located between New Jersey and Delaware. p. 67

Delaware River A river in the northeastern United States; begins in southern New York and flows into the Atlantic Ocean at Delaware Bay. p. 67

Delhi A city in northern India. (29°N, 77°E) p. 24

Denmark A country in central Europe; occupies the northern part of the Jutland Peninsula. p. 19

Denver Colorado's capital and largest city. (40°N, 105°W) p. 83

Des Moines (DUH•MOYN) Iowa's capital and largest city. (42°N, 94°W) p. 75

Deserts of the Arabian Peninsula A desert region in southwestern Asia on the Arabian Peninsula. p. 26

Detroit The largest city in Michigan; located on the Detroit River; center of the U.S. automobile industry. (42°N, 83°W) p. 75

Dismal Swamp A swamp that covers part of Virginia and North Carolina. p. 71

Djibouti (juh•BOO•tee) A country in East Africa. p. 22

Dominica An island nation in the Lesser Antilles between Guadeloupe and Martinique. p. 32

Dominican Republic A country in the Caribbean Islands, occupying the eastern part of the island of Hispaniola. p. 28

Dover The capital of Delaware. (39°N, 76°W) p. 67

Dublin The capital of the Republic of Ireland; located on the River Liffey, near Dublin Bay. (53°N, 6°W) p. 24

Duluth (duh•LOOTH) The third-largest city in Minnesota. (47°N, 92°W) p. 75

Durango A city in northwestern central Mexico. (24°N, 104°W) p. 28

E

East China Sea The part of the China Sea north of Taiwan. p. 27

Easter Island An island off the western coast of South America, in the Pacific Ocean. (27°S, 109°W) p. 18

Eastern Ghats A chain of mountains in southeast India. p. 26

Ecuador A country in northwestern South America, on the Pacific coast. p. 28

Edmonton The capital of Alberta, Canada; located in the south-central part of the province on both banks of the north Saskatchewan River. (53°N, 113°W) p. 30

Egypt (EE•juhpt) An ancient land and present-day country in northern Africa, on the coast of the Mediterranean and Red seas. p. 22

El Paso A city at the western tip of Texas; located on the Rio Grande. (32°N, 106°W) p. 79

El Salvador A Central American republic; located south of Guatemala, on the Pacific Ocean. p. 28

Ellesmere Island (ELZ•mir) The most northern of Canada's Arctic Islands. p. 29

English Channel An extension and connection of the Atlantic Ocean and the North Sea; south of the British Isles and north of France. p. 26

Equator An imaginary line that circles the Earth halfway between the North Pole and South Pole. The line divides the Earth into the Northern Hemisphere and the Southern Hemisphere. p. 20

Equatorial Guinea A country in West Africa. p. 22

Erie A city in northwestern Pennsylvania. (42°N, 80°W) p. 67

Erie Canal The longest canal in the world; part of the New York State Barge Canal System; connects Troy (on the Hudson River) with Buffalo (on Lake Erie). p. 67

Eritrea (air•uh•TREE•uh) A country on the Red Sea in North Africa, north of Ethiopia. p. 22

Estonia A country in northeastern Europe; formerly part of the Soviet Union. p. 19

Ethiopia A country in North Africa. p. 22

Euphrates River A river that begins in Turkey, flows through Syria and Iraq, and empties into the Persian Gulf. p. 26

Europe One of the world's seven continents. p. 19

European Plain A plains region that extends across most of Europe. p. 21

Everglades A large area of wetlands in southern Florida. p. 51

Everglades National Park A national park in southern Florida. p. 71

F

Fairbanks A city in central Alaska. (65°N, 148°W) p. 84

Falkland Islands A British colony in the Atlantic Ocean; located east of the Strait of Magellan. p. 28

Fès A sacred Muslim city in northern Morocco, near the Middle Atlas Mountains. (34°N, 5°W) p. 22

Fiji An island country in Melanesia, Oceania, in the southern Pacific Ocean. (17°S, 179°E) p. 34

Finger Lakes Located in west-central New York; near Seneca Falls. p. 51

Finland A country in northern Europe located east of Sweden. p. 19

Florida Keys A chain of islands off the southern tip of the Florida peninsula. p. 71

Formosa See Taiwan.

Fort Worth A city in northern Texas. (33°N, 97°W) p. 79

Fortaleza A city and port in northeastern Brazil. (3°S, 38°W) p. 28

Four Corners The point where four states — New Mexico, Colorado, Utah, and Arizona — meet. (37°N, 109°W) p. 79

France A country in western Europe p. 19

Frankfort The capital of Kentucky. (38°N, 85°W) p. 71

Fraser River A river that begins in the Rocky Mountains in Canada and empties into the Pacific Ocean near Vancouver, British Columbia. p. 30

French Guiana An overseas department of France, located on the northern Atlantic coast of South America. (4°N, 53°W) p. 28

Fresno A city in southern California. (37°N, 120°W) p. 86

G

Gabon A country in West Africa. p. 22

Galveston A city on Galveston Island, in Texas. (29°N, 95°W) p. 79

Galveston Bay A bay located on the Gulf of Mexico near Houston, Texas. p. 51

Ganges River (GAN•jeez) A river in India that flows into the Bay of Bengal. pp. 26 and 27

Gao (GOW) A trading center of the ancient Songhay Empire of West Africa; located on the Niger River in central Mali. (15°N, 4°W) p. 22

Gary A city in northwestern Indiana. (42°N, 87°W) p. 75

Gaza strip An area in southern Palestine, near the Mediterranean Sea. (32°N, 34°E) p. 24

Georgetown A city in South America located at the mouth of the Demerara River; capital of Guyana. (6°N, 58°W) p. 28

Georgia A country on the Black Sea in southeastern Europe; formerly part of the Soviet Union. p. 24

Germany A European country; located in northern central Europe. p. 19

Ghana (GAH•nuh) A country on the coast of West Africa; called the Gold Coast by Portuguese and Dutch colonizers. p. 22

Gila River (HEE•lah) A river in the southwestern United States. p. 79

Gobi (GOH•bee) (Desert) A desert in East Asia; located in Mongolia and China. p. 27

Grand Canyon A canyon in northwestern Arizona, formed by the Colorado River. p. 50

Grand Canyon National Park A national park in northwestern Arizona. p. 79

Grand Rapids A city in western Michigan. (43°N, 86°W) p. 75

Great Basin One of the driest parts of the United States; located in Nevada, Utah, California, Idaho, Wyoming, and Oregon; includes the Great Salt Lake Desert, the Mojave Desert, and Death Valley. p. 50

Great Britain A West European kingdom; includes England, Scotland, and Wales. (54°N, 2°W) p. 26

Great Lakes The largest group of freshwater lakes in the world; located in north-central North America. p. 51

Great Plains The western part of the Interior Plains of the United States. p. 51

Great Salt Lake The largest lake in the Great Basin, located in Utah. p. 50

Great Smoky Mountains National Park A national park on the Tennessee–North Carolina state line. p. 71

Greece An ancient center of civilization and present-day country in Europe; located on the southern end of the Balkan Peninsula. (40°N, 23°E) p. 19

Green Mountains A mountain range in the northeastern United States that extends from Canada through Vermont and into Massachusetts. p. 67

Greenland The largest island in the world; located in northeastern North America; a territory of Denmark. pp. 18 and 19

Greensboro A city in north-central North Carolina. (36°N, 80°W) p. 71

Guadalajara (gwah•duh•luh•HAR•uh) The capital of Jalisco state; located in central Mexico. (21°N, 103°W) p. 31

Guadalupe Mountains National Park (gwah•dah•LOO•pay) A national park near El Paso, Texas. p. 79

Guam (GWAHM) An unincorporated United States territory; largest and southernmost of the Mariana Islands; located in the western Pacific Ocean. (13°N, 145°E) p. 85

Guangzhou (GWAHNG•JOH) A Chinese port once known as Canton; located on the Zhu River in southeastern China. (23°N, 113°E) p. 25

Guatemala A former part of the Mayan Empire and later a colony of Spain; now an independent country in Central America. p. 28

Guatemala City A city in Central America; capital of Guatemala (the republic); largest city in Central America. (14°N, 90°W) p. 28

Guinea A country in West Africa. p. 22

Guinea-Bissau (gih•nee•bih•SOW) A former Portuguese province; now an independent country in West Africa. p. 22

Gulf of Bothnia An inlet of the Baltic Sea, between Sweden and Finland. p. 26

Gulf of California A part of the Pacific Ocean, located off northwestern Mexico. p. 29

Gulf of Guinea A gulf located on the western coast of Africa. p. 22

Gulf of Mexico A body of water off the southeastern coast of North America that is bounded by the United States, Cuba, and Mexico. p. 29

Gulf of Oman An arm of the Arabian Sea; located between northern Oman and the southeastern coast of Iran. p. 26

Gulf of St. Lawrence A deep gulf of the Atlantic Ocean, off the east coast of Canada, between Newfoundland and the Canadian mainland. p. 29

Gulf of Thailand An inlet of the South China Sea, between Malaysia and Thailand. p. 27

Gulf of Tonkin An inlet of the South China Sea, between Vietnam and China. p. 27

Guyana A country in the northern part of South America. p. 28

H

Hainan An island in the South China Sea; located southeast of China. (19°N, 110°E) p. 27

Haiti A country in the West Indies, occupying the western part of the island of Hispaniola. p. 28

Halifax The capital of the province of Nova Scotia, Canada; a major port on the Atlantic Ocean; remains free of ice all year. (44°N, 63°W) p. 30

Hamburg A city in northern Germany; located near the Elbe River and the North Sea. (54°N, 10°E) p. 24

Hanoi The capital of Vietnam; located on the northern Red River. (21°N, 106°E) p. 25

Harbin The capital of Heilungkiang province; located in northeastern China. p. 25

Harrisburg The captial of Pennsylvania. (40°N, 77°W) p. 67

Hartford The capital of Connecticut. (42°N, 73°W) p. 67

Havana The capital of Cuba. (23°N, 82°W) p. 28

Hawaii A state of the United States; the Hawaiian Islands are a chain of volcanic and coral islands in the northern central Pacific Ocean. (21°N, 156°W) p. 83

Hawaiian Islands A chain of volcanic and coral islands; located in the north-central Pacific Ocean. p. 84

Helena (HEH•luh•nuh) The capital of Montana. (46°N, 112°W) p. 83

Helsinki The capital city and port of Finland in Europe. (60°N, 125°E) p. 24

Herat The present-day name of an ancient city located in what is today northwestern Afghanistan. (34°N, 62°E) p. 24

Hilton Head Island An island off the coast of South Carolina. (32°N, 81°W) p. 71

Himalaya Mountains (hih•muh•LAY•uh) A mountain system on the northern edge of South Asia; runs through Nepal, Bhutan, southern Tibet, and northern India. pp. 26 and 27

Hindu Kush Mountains A mountain system that extends southwest from the Pamir Knot in eastern Tajikistan through northwestern Afghanistan. p. 26

Hispaniola (ees•pah•NYOH•lah) An island in the West Indies made up of Haiti and the Dominican Republic; located in the Caribbean Sea between Cuba and Puerto Rico. (19°N, 71°W) p. 29

Ho Chi Minh City A major city in Vietnam. (11°N, 107°E) p. 25

Hokkaido (hah•KYD•oh) The northernmost of the four main islands of Japan. (44°N, 143°E) p. 27

Honduras (ohn•DUR•ahs) A country in Central America; located west of the Caribbean Sea, north of Nicaragua, and east of Guatemala. p. 28

Hong Kong Long a British crown colony set to become part of China; located in southeastern China, south of Guangzhou. (22°N, 114°E) p. 25

Honolulu (hah•nuhl•OO•loo) Hawaii's capital and largest city. (21°N, 158°W) p. 83

Honshu The largest of the four main islands of Japan. (36°N, 138°E) p. 27

Hoover Dam A dam on the Colorado River on the Nevada–Arizona state line. (36°N, 114°W) p. 79

Hot Springs National Park A national park in the Ouachita Mountains in Arkansas. p. 71

Houston The largest city in Texas; third-largest port in the United States; leading industrial center in Texas. (30°N, 95°W) p. 79

Huang He (HWAHNG HUH) A river that flows from the Plateau of Tibet in China. p. 27

Hudson Bay A bay located in northern Canada; borders the Northwest Territories, Manitoba, Ontario, and Quebec; reaches the Atlantic Ocean through the Hudson Strait. p. 29

Hudson River A river in the northeastern United States beginning in upper New York and flowing into the Atlantic Ocean; named for the explorer Henry Hudson. p. 67

Hudson Strait A strait between southern Baffin Island and northern Quebec, in northeastern Canada; connects the Atlantic Ocean with Hudson Bay. p. 29

Hungary A country in central Europe. p. 19

Huntsville A city in northern Alabama. (35°N, 86°W) p. 71

Hyderabad A former Indian state; land absorbed by the states of Andhra Pradesh, Mysore, and Maharashtra; located in central India. p. 24

I

Iberian Peninsula A peninsula forming southwestern Europe; extends into the Atlantic Ocean and the Mediterranean Sea; occupied by the countries of Portugal and Spain. p. 26

Iceland A European island country in the northern Atlantic Ocean; located southeast of Greenland. (65°N, 19°W) p. 26

Illinois River A river in Illinois; flows southwest into the Mississippi River. p. 75

Illinois Waterway A waterway that connects Lake Michigan with the Illinois River. p. 75

India A country in South Asia; occupies much of a large peninsula extending from central Asia into the Indian Ocean. pp. 24 and 25

Indian Ocean One of the world's four oceans. p. 21

Indianapolis (ihn•dee•uh•NA•puh•luhs) The capital of Indiana. (40°N, 86°W) p. 75

Indonesia A country in Southeast Asia. p. 25

Indus River A river in South Asia; flows from Tibet, through northern India and Pakistan, and into the Arabian Sea. p. 26

Interior Plains One of two major plains in the United States; located between the Appalachian Mountains and the Rocky Mountains; includes the Central Plains and the Great Plains. p. 51

Ionian Sea The sea located east of Italy and west of Greece. p. 26

Iran A country in Southwest Asia; formerly known as Persia; located on the Persian Gulf. p. 24

Iraq A country in Southwest Asia; includes former lands of the Mesopotamians, Babylonians, Sumerians, and Assyrians. p. 24

Ireland A country of Europe, located on the British Isles. p. 24

Irkutsk (ir•KOOTSK) A city located in Irkutsk Oblast, Russia, on the shore of Lake Baikal. (58°N, 104°E) p. 25

Irrawaddy River A river in southern central Burma (Myanmar). p. 27

Islamabad The capital of Pakistan. (34°N, 73°E) p. 24

Isle Royale National Park A national park near the northwestern shores of Lake Superior. p. 75

Israel (IZ•ree•uhl) An ancient kingdom and present-day country; a holy land for Jews, Christians, and Muslims; located on the eastern coast of the Mediterranean Sea. p. 24

Isthmus of Panama (IHS•muhs) A narrow land bridge containing the country of Panama; located between the Caribbean Sea and the Pacific Ocean; connects Central and South America. p. 29

Italian Peninsula A boot-shaped peninsula extending from southern central Europe into the Mediterranean Sea; occupied by Italy. p. 26

Italy An ancient center of civilization and present-day European country; located on the Italian Peninsula. p. 24

J

Jackson The capital of Mississippi. (32°N, 90°W) p. 71

Jacksonville A city in northeastern Florida; located near the mouth of the St. Johns River. (30°N, 82°W) p. 71

Jamaica (juh•MAY•kuh) An island country in the West Indies, south of Cuba. p. 28

James River A river in central Virginia; begins where the Jackson and Cowpasture rivers join; flows into Chesapeake Bay. p. 71

Jamestown The first permanent English settlement in the Americas; located on the shore of the James River. (37°N, 76°W) p. 58

Japan A country in East Asia; consists of Honshu, Hokkaido, Kyushu, Shikoku, and other islands in the western Pacific Ocean. p. 25

Java The most important island of Indonesia; located in southern Indonesia. (7°S, 110°E) p. 27

Java Sea Part of the Pacific Ocean north of Java, south of Borneo, and east of Sumatra. p. 27

Jefferson City The capital of Missouri. (39°N, 92°W) p. 75

Jersey City A port city in northeastern New Jersey. (41°N, 74°W) p. 67

Jerusalem The capital of Israel; a holy city for Jews, Christians, and Muslims. (32°N, 35°E) p. 24

Johannesburg A city located in the country of South Africa. (26°S, 28°E) p. 22

Jordan A country in Southwest Asia. p. 24

Juneau (JOO•noh) The capital of Alaska. (58°N, 134°W) p. 83

Jutland A peninsula occupied by the mainland of Denmark. p. 26

K

Kahoolawe (kah•hoh•uh•LAY•vay) One of the eight main islands of Hawaii; located west of Maui. p. 84

Kalahari Desert A desert in southern Africa; located in Botswana, Namibia, and South Africa. p. 23

Kamchatka Peninsula A peninsula in northeastern Russia; surrounded by the Sea of Okhotsk and the Bering Sea. (57°N, 160°E) p. 27

Kanpur A city in northern India; located on the Ganges River, southeast of Delhi. (26°N, 80°E) p. 24

Kansas City The largest city in Missouri; located on the Missouri River on the Kansas-Missouri border. (39°N, 95°W) p. 75

Karachi A city and seaport, former capital of Pakistan; located northwest of the Indus River mouth. (25°N, 67°E) p. 24

Kathmandu The capital of Nepal on the Indian subcontinent; located in the valley of the Himalayas. (27°N, 85°E) p. 25

Kauai (KAU•eye) The fourth largest of the eight major Hawaiian islands. p. 84

Kazakhstan (ka•zak•STAN) A country in Central Asia; formerly part of the Soviet Union. p. 24

Kennebec River (KEH•nih•bek) A river in west-central and southern Maine; flows south from Moosehead Lake to the Atlantic Ocean. p. 67

Kenya A country in East Africa. p. 22

Kiev (KEE•ef) The capital of Ukraine; located on the Dnieper River, in central Ukraine. (50°N, 31°E) p. 24

Kingston A commercial seaport in the West Indies; capital of Jamaica. (18°N, 76°W) p. 28

Kodiak Island (KOH•dee•ah) An island in the Gulf of Alaska. p. 84

Korea An East Asian country now divided into North and South Korea; occupies a peninsula on the eastern coast of China. p. 25

Kunlun Shan (KOON•LOON SHAN) A mountain range in western China. pp. 26 and 27

Kuwait An independent state on the northwestern Persian Gulf; located between Iraq and Saudi Arabia. (30°N, 48°E) p. 24

Kyrgyzstan (kir•gi•STAN) A country in Central Asia; formerly part of the Soviet Union. p. 24

Kyushu (kee•OO•shoo) The southernmost of the four main islands of Japan. (33°N, 131°E) p. 27

L

La Paz A city in South America; capital of Bolivia. (16°S, 68°W) p. 28

Labrador The northeastern tip of North America; once known as Markland. p. 29

Lake Athabasca A lake located in Canada, in northeastern Alberta and northwestern Saskatchewan. p. 29

Lake Chad A lake in northern Africa on the border of Chad, Cameroon, Nigeria, and Niger. p. 23

Lake Champlain (sham•PLAYN) A large lake on the New York–Vermont state line. p. 67

Lake Erie The fourth largest of the Great Lakes, bordering New York, Pennsylvania, Ohio, Michigan, and Canada. p. 51

Lake Huron The second largest of the Great Lakes, bordering Michigan and Canada. p. 51

Lake Malawi A large lake along the eastern border of Malawi in southern Africa; also called Lake Nyasa. p. 23

Lake Mead A reservoir on the Colorado River, formed by Hoover Dam. p. 79

Lake Michigan The third largest of the Great Lakes, the only one entirely within the United States. p. 51

Lake Okeechobee (oh•kuh•CHOH•bee) The largest lake in the southern United States, located in south Florida along the northern edge of the Everglades. p. 71

Lake Ontario The smallest of the Great Lakes; borders Canada and New York. p. 51

Lake Powell A human-made lake in Glen Canyon National Recreation Area in southern Utah. p. 50

Lake Superior The largest of the Great Lakes, bordering Michigan, Wisconsin, Minnesota, and Canada. p. 51

Lake Tanganyika (tang•uhn•YEE•kuh) A lake in Tanzania and Democratic Republic of Congo, in the Great Rift Valley of southern Africa. p. 23

Lake Titicaca (tih•tih•KAH•kah) The highest navigable lake in the world; located on the border between Peru and Bolivia. p. 29

Lake Victoria A lake in Tanzania, Kenya, and Uganda in southeastern Africa. p. 23

Lake Winnipeg A lake located in Manitoba. p. 29

Lanai (luh•NY) An island in central Hawaii located west of Maui; a major pineapple-producing area. p. 84

Lansing The capital of Michigan. (43°N, 85°W) p. 75

Laos A country on the Indochina Peninsula in Southeast Asia; once part of former French Indochina. p. 25

Las Vegas A city in the southeastern corner of Nevada. (36°N, 115°W) p. 83

Latvia A country in eastern Europe; formerly part of the Soviet Union. p. 24

Lebanon The land of the ancient Phoenicians and present-day country on the eastern shore of the Mediterranean Sea in Southwest Asia. p. 24

Leningrad See St. Petersburg.

León A city in central Mexico; located northwest of Guanajuato. (21°N, 102°W) p. 31

Lesotho An independent country located within the borders of the country of South Africa in Africa. (30°S, 28°E) p. 22

Lexington A city in north-central Kentucky. (38°N, 84°W) p. 71

Liberia A country in West Africa; originally a republic for freed slaves from the United States; located on the Atlantic coast of West Africa. p. 22

Libya A country in northern Africa; located on the Mediterranean Sea. p. 22

Libyan Desert A desert in northern Africa; located in Libya, Egypt, and Sudan. p. 23

Lima (LEE•muh) The capital of Peru; located on the Rimac River. (12°S, 77°W) p. 28

Lincoln The capital of Nebraska. (41°N, 97°W) p. 75

Lisbon The capital of Portugal; located on the Atlantic coast of Europe. (39°N, 9°W) p. 24

Lithuania A country in eastern Europe; formerly part of the Soviet Union. p. 24

Little Rock The capital of Arkansas. (35°N, 92°W) p. 71

London The capital of the United Kingdom; located on the Thames River, in southeast England. (51°N, 0°) p. 24

Long Beach A port city in southwestern California. (34°N, 118°W) p. 86

Long Island An island located east of New York City and south of Connecticut; lies between Long Island Sound and the Atlantic Ocean. p. 67

Long Island Sound The body of water separating Connecticut and Long Island, New York. p. 68

Los Angeles The largest city in California; the second-largest city in the United States. (34°N, 118°W) p. 83

Louisville (LOO•ih•vil) The largest city in Kentucky; located on the Ohio River. (38°N, 86°W) p. 71

Luxembourg A medieval county and duchy; now largely in the Grand Duchy of Luxembourg and the Belgian province of Luxembourg. p. 24

M

Macao (muh•KOW) A Portuguese colony in southern China, on the South China Sea. (22°N, 114°E) p. 25

Macedonia A country in eastern Europe; located on lands that were part of the former Yugoslavia. p. 24

Mackenzie River A river located in western Mackenzie district, Northwest Territories, Canada; flows north-northwest into Mackenzie Bay; second longest river in North America. p. 29

Macon (MAY•kuhn) A city in central Georgia; located on the Ocmulgee River, southeast of Atlanta. (33°N, 84°W) p. 71

Madagascar An island country in the Indian Ocean, off the eastern coast of southern Africa. (20°S, 47°E) p. 22

Madison The capital of Wisconsin. (43°N, 89°W) p. 75

Madras See Chennai.

Madrid A city located in central Spain, in Europe, on the Manzanares River. (40°N, 4°W) p. 24

Majorca (mah•YOR•kah) The largest island of the Balearic group, in Spain. (40°N, 3°E) p. 26

Malawi A country in southeastern Africa. p. 22

Malay Peninsula A peninsula in Southeast Asia, divided between Thailand and Malaysia. p. 27

Malaysia An independent federation; located in southeastern Asia. (5°N, 110°E) p. 25

Mali A former West African empire and present-day country. p. 22

Mammoth Cave National Park A national park in south-central Kentucky. p. 71

Managua A city in Central America; capital of Nicaragua; located on the south shore of Lake Managua. (12°N, 86°W) p. 28

Manaus A city located in western Brazil on the left bank of Rio Negro. (3°S, 60°W) p. 28

Manitoba A province in central Canada. p. 30

Marquesas Islands (mar•KAY•zuhz) A group of ten islands of French Polynesia; located in the southern Pacific Ocean. (10°S, 140°W) p. 34

Marrakech A city near the Grand Atlas Mountains, in Morocco. (32°N, 8°W) p. 22

Marshall Islands A group of 32 islands and more than 867 reefs; located in the western Pacific Ocean. (9°N, 171°E) p. 34

Massachusetts Bay An inlet of the Atlantic Ocean on the east coast of Massachusetts; extends from Cape Ann to Cape Cod. p. 67

Matamoros (mah•tah•MOH•rohs) A city in northeastern Mexico. (26°N, 97°W) p. 31

Maui (MOW•ee) The second largest of the eight major Hawaiian islands. p. 84

Mauritania (maw•ruh•TAY•nee•uh) A country in West Africa. p. 22

Mauritius (maw•RIH•shuhs) An island of the Mascarene Islands; located in the Indian Ocean. (20°S, 57°E) p. 19

Mecca (MEH•kuh) A city in Saudi Arabia near the Red Sea; a holy city for Muslims. (22°N, 40°E) p. 24

Medina A city in western Saudi Arabia (25°N, 40°E) p. 24

Mediterranean Sea (meh•duh•tuh•RAY•nee•uhn) The sea south of Europe, north of Africa, and west of Asia; connects to the Atlantic Ocean, the Red Sea, and the Black Sea. p. 26

Mekong River One of the chief rivers of Southeast Asia; flows from the mountains of Tibet into the South China Sea. (10°N, 106°E) p. 27

Melanesia (meh•luh•NEE•zhuh) The name given to a region of Pacific islands; located northeast of Australia and south of the equator. p. 21

Memphis A city in the southwestern corner of Tennessee, on the Mississippi River. (35°N, 90°W) p. 71

Mesa Verde (MAY•suh VAIR•day) An ancient settlement of the Anasazi; located in southwestern Colorado. p. 83

Mesabi Range (muh•SAH•bee) An area of low hills in northeastern Minnesota. p. 75

Mexico A country in southern North America; located between the United States and Central America. p. 18

Mexico City The capital of Mexico and of the Federal District; located in central Mexico. (19°N, 99°W) p. 28

Miami A city in southeastern Florida, on Biscayne Bay. (25°N, 80°W) p. 71

Micronesia (my•kruh•NEE•zhuh) The name given to a region of Pacific islands; located east of the Philippines and north of the equator. p. 21

Middle America A world region; includes Mexico, the countries of Central America, and sometimes the islands of the Caribbean Sea. p. 57

Middle West Region One of the five regions of the United States. p. 65

Midway Islands A United States territory in the Pacific Ocean. p. 18

Milan A city in northern Italy. (45°N, 9°E) p. 24

Milwaukee (mil•WAH•kee) The largest city in Wisconsin; located on Lake Michigan. (43°N, 88°W) p. 75

Minneapolis The largest city in Minnesota; located on the Mississippi River; twin city with St. Paul. (45°N, 93°W) p. 75

Mississippi River The largest river in the United States; flows from Minnesota to the Gulf of Mexico. p. 51

Missouri River A tributary of the Mississippi River; flows from Montana to St. Louis, Missouri. p. 51

Mobile (moh•BEEL) A seaport in Alabama; located at the mouth of the Mobile River. (31°N, 88°W) p. 71

Mobile Bay An inlet of the Gulf of Mexico; the site of a Civil War naval battle in 1864. p. 72

Mogadishu (mah•guh•DIH•shoo) A port on the Indian Ocean in southern Somalia in Africa. (2°N, 45°E) p. 22

Moldova A country in eastern Europe; formerly part of the Soviet Union. (47°N, 27°E) p. 24

Molokai (mah•luh•KY) A Hawaiian island. p. 84

Mombasa An island port on the coast of the Indian Ocean, in southern Kenya in Africa. (4°S, 40°E) p. 22

Mongolia Known as the Mongolian People's Republic; located in East Asia, south of Russia and north of China. p. 25

Monongahela River (muh•nahn•guh•HEE•luh) A river in northern West Virginia and southwestern Pennsylvania; flows north across the Pennsylvania border and at Pittsburgh joins with the Allegheny River to form the Ohio River. p. 67

Monterrey The capital of Nuevo León state; located in northeastern Mexico. (26°N, 100°W) p. 31

Montevideo A seaport city located in the southern part of the north shore of La Plata estuary; capital of Uruguay. (35°S, 56°W) p. 28

Montgomery The capital of Alabama. (32°N, 86°W) p. 71

Montpelier (mawnt•PEEL•yer) The capital of Vermont. (44°N, 73°W) p. 67

Montreal The largest city and chief port of entry in Canada; located in the province of Quebec, in the St. Lawrence lowlands. (45°N, 73°W) p. 30

Morocco A country in North Africa; bordered by the Mediterranean Sea and the Atlantic Ocean. p. 22

Moscow The capital of Russia; located on the Moscow River. (56°N, 38°E) p. 24

Mount McKinley The highest mountain in North America, located in central Alaska. (64°N, 150°W) p. 50

Mount Rainier (ruh•NIR) The highest mountain in the Cascade Range. (47°N, 103°W) p. 50

Mount Rushmore A mountain in the Black Hills of South Dakota. (44°N, 103°W) p. 75

Mount St. Helens A volcano in the Cascade Range that erupted in 1980. (47°N, 122°W) p. 85

Mount Washington A mountain in the White Mountains of New Hampshire. (44°N, 71°W) p. 67

Mozambique (moh•zuhm•BEEK) A country in southern Africa; formerly Portuguese East Africa. p. 22

Mumbai See Bombay.

Munich A city in southeastern Germany. (48°N, 12°E) p. 24

N

Nagoya (nah•GOY•ah) A Japanese industrial city on the coast of Honshu in southern Japan. (35°N, 136°E) p. 25

Namibia A country in southwestern Africa; a territory governed by South Africa until 1990. (22°S, 18°E) p. 22

Naples An Italian port on the Tyrrhenian Sea; located on the western coast of southern Italy. (41°N, 14°E) p. 24

Narmada River A sacred Hindu river; begins in eastern India, and empties into the Gulf of Cambay. p. 26

Nashville The capital of Tennessee. (36°N, 87°W) p. 71

Nassau A city on the northeastern coast of New Providence Island; capital of the Bahama Islands. (25°N, 77°W) p. 28

Nepal A country located in South Asia, on the Indian subcontinent. p. 25

Netherlands A country on the northern coast of central Europe, on the North Sea. p. 24

New Brunswick One of Canada's ten provinces. p. 30

New Delhi The capital of India; located in northern India. (29°N, 77°E) p. 24

New Guinea (GIH•nee) An island of the eastern Malay Archipelago; located in the western Pacific Ocean, north of Australia; second-largest island in the world. p. 27

New Haven A city in southern Connecticut on New Haven Harbor. (41°N, 73°W) p. 67

New Orleans (AWR•lee•uhns) The largest city in Louisiana; a major port located between the Mississippi River and Lake Pontchartrain. (30°N, 90°W) p. 71

New York City The largest city in the United States; located in southeastern New York at the mouth of the Hudson River. (41°N, 74°W) p. 67

New York State Barge Canal System A system of canals that links the Great Lakes with the Hudson River and the Atlantic Ocean. p. 67

New Zealand An island-group country in the southwestern Pacific Ocean, southeast of Australia. (40°S, 176°E) p. 34

Newark A port in northeastern New Jersey on the Passaic River and Newark Bay. (41°N, 74°W) p. 67

Newfoundland One of Canada's ten provinces. p. 30

Niagara Falls (ny•AG•ruh) The large waterfalls on the Niagara River. (43°N, 79°W) p. 67

Nicaragua A country in Central America. p. 28

Niger A country in West Africa. p. 22

Niger River A river in West Africa; flows from Guinea through Mali, Niger, and Nigeria into the Gulf of Guinea. p. 23

Nigeria (ny•JIR•ee•uh) A former territory of the Portuguese; country on the Gulf of Guinea, in West Africa. p. 22

Niihau (NEE•how) A Hawaiian island, located southwest of Kauai. p. 84

Nile River A river in northeastern Africa; flows from Lake Victoria to the Mediterranean Sea at the northeastern coast of Egypt; the longest river in the world. p. 23

Nome A city on the southern side of the Seward Peninsula; located in western Alaska. (65°N, 165°W) p. 84

Norfolk (NAWR•fawk) A city in southeastern Virginia; located on the Elizabeth River. (37°N, 76°W) p. 71

North America One of the world's seven continents. p. 18

North American Desert A desert region in western North America. p. 37

North Borneo The British colonial name of Sabah; a state of Malaysia; located in northeastern Borneo. p. 25

North Korea A country in eastern Asia. p. 25

North Pole The northernmost point on the Earth. (90°N) p. 20

North Sea A part of the Atlantic Ocean, located east of Great Britain and west of Denmark. p. 26

Northeast Region One of the five regions of the United States. p. 65

Northwest Territories One of Canada's three territories. p. 30

Norway A European country; located on the northwestern Scandinavian Peninsula. p. 24

Nova Scotia (noh•vuh SKOH•shuh) One of Canada's ten provinces; located on a peninsula. p. 30

Novgorod (NAHV•guh•rahd) A medieval principality in eastern Europe in what is present-day Russia. (58°N, 31°E) p. 24

Nubian Desert A desert region in Sudan, Africa; east of the Nile River. (22°N, 34°E) p. 23

Nunavut Territory One of Canada's three territories. p. 30

O

Oahu (oh•AH•hoo) The third-largest of eight main islands of Hawaii; Honolulu is located there. p. 84

Ocmulgee River (ohk•MUHL•gee) A river in central Georgia; formed by the junction of the Yellow and South rivers, flows south and southeast to join the Oconee River and then forms the Altamaha River. p. 71

Ohio River A tributary of the Mississippi River; begins in Pittsburgh, Pennsylvania, and ends in Cairo, Illinois. p. 51

Okefenokee Swamp (oh•kee•fuh•NOH•kee) A swamp that covers part of southeastern Georgia and northern Florida. p. 71

Okinawa An island group; center of Ryukyu Islands between the East China Sea and the Pacific Ocean. (27°N, 128°E) p. 25

Oklahoma City The capital of Oklahoma. (35°N, 98°W) p. 79

Olympia (oh•LIM•pee•uh) The capital of Washington. (47°N, 123°W) p. 83

Omaha The largest city in Nebraska; located on the Missouri River. (41°N, 96°W) p. 75

Oman A country located on the Arabian Peninsula on the Gulf of Oman in Southwest Asia. p. 24

Ontario One of Canada's ten provinces. p. 30

Orinoco River A river in Venezuela; flows west then north forming a section of the Colombia-Venezuela boundary, then turns east in central Venezuela and empties through a wide delta into the Atlantic Ocean. p. 29

Orlando A city in central Florida. (28°N, 81°W) p. 71

Osaka A Japanese port in southern Honshu where the Yodo River meets Osaka Bay. (35°N, 136°E) p. 25

Oslo The capital of Norway; located in southeastern Norway at the northern end of the Oslo Fjord. (60°N, 11°E) p. 24

Ottawa (AH•tuh•wuh) The capital of Canada; located in Ontario on the St. Lawrence Lowlands. (45°N, 75°W) p. 30

Ouachita Mountains (WAH•shuh•tah) A mountain range in western Arkansas and southeastern Oklahoma. p. 51

Outer Banks A chain of sand islands and peninsulas along the coast of North Carolina. p. 71

Ozark Plateau (OH•zahrk) A plateau extending from southeastern Missouri across Arkansas and into eastern Oklahoma. p. 51

P

Pacific Ocean The largest of the world's four oceans. pp. 20 and 21

Painted Desert A desert region in Arizona. p. 79

Pakistan A country in South Asia. p. 24

Pampa (PAHM•puh) A plains region in central South America. p. 29

Panama The southernmost country in Central America. (9°N, 79°W) p. 28

Panama Canal A canal across the Isthmus of Panama; extends from the Caribbean Sea to the Gulf of Panama. p. 18

Panama City A city in Central America; capital of the Republic of Panama. (9°N, 79°W) p. 28

Paraguay A country in central South America; former colony of Spain. p. 28

Paraguay River A river in south-central South America; empties into the Paraná at the southwestern corner of Paraguay. p. 29

Paramaribo A seaport city located on the Suriname River; capital of Suriname. (5°N, 55°W) p. 28

Paraná River A river in southeast-central South America; formed by the joining of the Rio Grande and the Paranaíba River in south-central Brazil. p. 29

Paris The capital of France; located on the Seine River. (49°N, 2°E) p. 24

Peace River A river in western Canada; flows east across border of Alberta, turns northeast and joins the Slave River just north of its outlet from Lake Athabasca. p. 29

Pearl Harbor An inlet on the southern coast of Oahu island, Hawaii; site of the Japanese bombing attack that brought the United States into World War II. p. 84

Pecos River (PAY•kohs) A river in eastern New Mexico and western Texas; empties into the Rio Grande. p. 79

Persian Gulf A gulf in Southwest Asia; connected to the Gulf of Oman and the Arabian Sea. p. 26

Peru A country on the Pacific coast of South America; former center of the Inca Empire. p. 28

Petrified Forest National Park A national park in eastern Arizona. p. 79

Philadelphia A city in southeastern Pennsylvania; located where the Delaware and Schuylkill rivers meet; major U.S. port. (40°N, 75°W) p. 67

Philippine Islands A group of more than 7,000 islands off the coast of Southeast Asia, making up the country of the Philippines. p. 27

Philippine Sea The part of the western Pacific Ocean east of the Philippines. p. 27

Philippines A country in Southeast Asia; located east of the Indochina Peninsula. (12°N, 123E°) p. 25

Phnom Penh (NAHM PEN) The capital of Cambodia. (12°N, 105°E) p. 25

Phoenix (FEE•niks) The capital of Arizona. (33°N, 112°W) p. 79

Piedmont (PEED•mahnt) A region of high land that lies east of the Appalachian Mountains. p. 51

Pierre (PIR) The capital of South Dakota. (44°N, 100°W) p. 75

Pittsburgh The second-largest city in Pennsylvania; the Allegheny and Monongahela rivers meet there to form the Ohio River. (40°N, 80°W) p. 67

Platte River (PLAT) A river in central Nebraska; flows east into the Missouri River below Omaha. p. 51

Plymouth (PLIH•muhth) A town on Plymouth Bay in Massachusetts; the site of the first settlement built by Pilgrims who sailed on the *Mayflower*. (42°N, 71°W) *p.* 67

Pocono Mountains (POH•kuh•noh) A mountain range in eastern Pennsylvania. p. 67

Polynesia (pah•luh•NEE•zhuh) The name given to a region of Pacific islands; includes New Zealand, Samoa, Tahiti, and the Hawaiian Islands. p. 20

Port-au-Prince A seaport located in Hispaniola Island, in the West Indies, on the southeastern shore of the Gulf of Gonave; capital of Haiti. (18°N, 72°W) p. 28

Portland (ME) A seaport city in southwestern Maine. (44°N, 70°W) p. 67

Portland (OR) Oregon's largest city. (46°N, 123°W) p. 83

Porto A port city located in northwestern Portugal, on the Douro River. (40°N, 9°W) p. 24

Pôrto Alegre A seaport city in southern Brazil; located on an inlet at the northern end of Lagoa dos Patos. p. 28

Portugal A country in Europe. (40°N, 8°W) p. 24

Portuguese Guinea A colony on the West African coast; formerly controlled by Portugal; the present-day country of Guinea-Bissau. p. 22

Potomac River (puh•TOH•muhk) A river on the Coastal Plain of the United States; begins in West Virginia and flows into Chesapeake Bay; Washington, D.C., is located on this river. p. 71

Prague The capital of the Czech Republic; located on both sides of the Vltava River. (50°N, 14°E) p. 24

Pretoria The administrative capital of the Republic of South Africa. (26°S, 28°E) p. 22

Prime meridian An imaginary line that divides the Earth into the Eastern Hemisphere and the Western Hemisphere. p. 11

Prince Edward Island One of Canada's ten provinces. p. 30

Principe (PRIN•suh•puh) Equatorial island; located off West Africa, in the Gulf of Guinea. (0°, 7°E) p. 23

Providence (PRAW•vuh•duhns) The capital and largest city of Rhode Island. (42°N, 71°W) p. 67

Puebla A city in southeastern central Mexico. (19°N, 98°W) p. 28

Pueblo (PWEH•bloh) A city in Colorado. p. 83

Puerto Rico (PWAIR•tuh REE•koh) A commonwealth of the United States, located southeast of Florida, in the Caribbean Sea. p. 72

P'yongyang (pee•AWNG•yahng) The capital of North Korea; located on the Taedong River. (39°N, 126°E) p. 25

Pyrenees Mountains The mountain range that separates the Iberian Peninsula from Europe; forms the border between Spain and France. p. 26

Q

Quebec (kwih•BEK) The capital of the province of Quebec, in Canada; located on the north side of the St. Lawrence River; the first successful French settlement in the Americas; established in 1608. (46°N, 71°W) p. 30

Quebec One of Canada's ten provinces. p. 30

Quito (KEE•toh) A city in South America; lies almost on the equator, just southeast of the volcano Pichincha; capital of Ecuador. (0°S, 78°W) p. 28

R

Raleigh (RAH•lee) The capital of North Carolina. (36°N, 79°W) p. 71

Rangoon The capital of Burma (Myanmar). (17°N, 96°E) p. 25

Recife A seaport located in eastern Brazil at the mouth of the Capibaribe River near Point Plata. (8°S, 35°W) p. 28

Red River A tributary of the Mississippi River; rises in eastern New Mexico, flows across Louisiana and into the Mississippi River; forms much of the Texas-Oklahoma border. p. 51

Red Sea The long, narrow sea between northeastern

Africa and the Arabian Peninsula; connected to the Mediterranean Sea by the Suez Canal and to the Arabian Sea by the Gulf of Aden. p. 26

Regina (rih•JY•nuh) The capital of Saskatchewan, Canada; located in the southern part of the province. (50°N, 104°W) p. 30

Reno (REE•noh) The second-largest city in Nevada. (40°N, 120°W) p. 83

Rhine River A river in western Europe; flows across Switzerland, western Germany, and the Netherlands to the North Sea. p. 26

Richmond The capital of Virginia; located on the Fall Line of the James River. (38°N, 77°W) p. 71

Riga The capital of the country of Latvia in eastern Europe. (57°N, 24°E) p. 24

Rio de Janeiro A commercial seaport in southeastern Brazil on the southwest shore of Guanabara Bay. (23°S, 43°W) p. 28

Rio de la Plata A river on the southeastern coast of South America. p. 29

Rio Grande The river that forms the Texas-Mexico border. p. 29

Roanoke River (ROH•uh•nohk) A river in southern Virginia and northeastern North Carolina; flows east and southeast across the North Carolina border and continues southeast into Albemarle Sound. p. 71

Rochester (RAH•ches•ter) A port city located in western New York. (43°N, 78°W) p. 67

Rocky Mountains A range of mountains covering much of the United States and Canada and extending from Alaska to New Mexico; these mountains divide rivers that flow east from those that flow west. p. 50

Romania A country in southeast Europe, bordering the Black Sea. p. 24

Rome The capital of the ancient Roman Empire and of present-day Italy; located on the Tiber River. (42°N, 11°E) p. 24

Russia A country in northeastern Europe and northern Asia; a historic empire and the largest republic of the former Soviet Union. p. 19

Rwanda A country in East Africa. p. 22

S

Sabine River (sah•BEEN) A river in Texas. p. 79

Sacramento (sak•ruh•MEN•toh) The capital of California. (39°N, 121°W) p. 83

Sacramento River A river in northwestern California. p. 83

Sahara (suh•HAIR•uh) A desert region in northern Africa. p. 23

Salem (SAY•luhm) The capital of Oregon. (45°N, 123°W) p. 83

Salt Lake City Utah's capital and largest city; located on the Jordan River. (41°N, 112°W) p. 83

Salvador A seaport city in eastern Brazil, located on All Saints Bay. (13°S, 38°W) p. 28

Samoa A group of Pacific islands in southwestern

Polynesia. (14°S, 171°W) p. 34

San Antonio A city in central Texas; located on the San Antonio River; the Alamo is located there. (29°N, 99°W) p. 79

San Diego A large city on the coast of southern California. (33°N, 117°W) p. 83

San Francisco The largest city in northern California; located on San Francisco Bay. (38°N, 123°W) p. 83

San Joaquin River (wah•KEEN) A river in central California. p. 83

San Jose (hoh•ZAY) A city in western California. (37°N, 122°W) p. 83

San José A city in Central America; capital of Costa Rica. (10°N, 84°W) p. 28

San Juan (san WAHN) Puerto Rico's capital and largest city. (18°N, 66°W) p. 72

San Marino A small country on Mount Titano within northern Italy. (44°N, 12°E) p. 24

San Salvador The capital of El Salvador. (13°N, 58°W) p. 28

Santa Fe (san•tah FAY) The capital of New Mexico. (36°N, 106°W) p. 79

Santo Domingo A city and the capital of the Dominican Republic. (18°N, 70°W) p. 28

São Francisco River A river in eastern Brazil; flows north, northeast, and east into the Atlantic Ocean south of Maceió. p. 29

São Paulo A city in southeastern Brazil; capital of São Paulo state. p. 28

São Tomé and Príncipe (SOW tuh•MAY PRIN•suh•puh) Island country off the coast of West Africa. p. 22

Sapporo A Japanese city. (0°, 141°E) p. 25

Sarajevo (sair•uh•YAY•voh) A city in central Bosnia and Herzegovina. (44°N, 18°E) p. 24

Sardinia An Italian island in the Mediterranean Sea; located west of the central coast. (40°N, 9°E) p. 26

Saskatchewan (suh•SKA•chuh•wahn) One of Canada's ten provinces. p. 30

Saskatchewan River A river located in southwestern and south-central Canada; flows from the Rocky Mountains east into north Lake Winnipeg. p. 29

Saudi Arabia A country that occupies most of the Arabian Peninsula in Southwest Asia. p. 24

Sault Sainte Marie A city in northern Michigan; located at the falls on St. Mary's river. (46°N, 84°W) p. 75

Savannah (suh•VA•nuh) The oldest city in Georgia; located at the mouth of the Savannah River. (32°N, 81°W) p. 71

Savannah River A river that forms the border between Georgia and South Carolina; flows into the Atlantic Ocean at Savannah, Georgia. p. 71

Scranton (SKRAN•tuhn) A city in northeastern Pennsylvania. (41°N, 76°W) p. 67

Sea of Japan The sea located west of Japan and east of Russia, North Korea, and South Korea; known in Korea as the East Sea. p. 27

Seattle (see•AT•uhl) The largest city in Washington State; located on Puget Sound. (48°N, 122°W) p. 83

Senegal A country in West Africa p. 22

Senegal River A river in West Africa; flows from the highlands of Guinea into the Atlantic Ocean at Senegal. p. 23

Seoul The capital of South Korea; located on the Han River. (38°N, 127°E) p. 25

Serbia Part of the former Yugoslavia. (44°N, 21°E) p. 24

Shanghai (shang•HY) A port on the East China Sea; located near the mouth of the Chang Jiang. (31°N, 121°E) p. 25

Shenandoah National Park (shehn•uhn•DOH•uh) A national park in the Blue Ridge Mountains, in northern Virginia. p. 71

Shikoku The smallest of the four main islands of Japan; located south of Honshu. (34°N, 134°E) p. 27

Sicily An Italian island off the southwestern tip of the Italian Peninsula. (38°N, 15°E) p. 26

Sierra Leone A country on the Atlantic coast of West Africa; a former slave colony. p. 22

Sierra Madre Occidental (see•EH•rah MAH•dray ahk•sih•den•TAHL) A mountain range in western Mexico, running parallel to the Pacific coast. p. 29

Sierra Madre Oriental A mountain range in eastern Mexico, along the coast of the Gulf of Mexico. p. 29

Sierra Nevada The mountain range in eastern California that runs parallel to the Coast Ranges. p. 83

Sinai Peninsula The peninsula between northeastern Africa and Southwest Asia; part of the country of Egypt. (30°N, 34°E) p. 26

Singapore A small island country off the southern tip of the Malay Peninsula, in Southeast Asia. (1°N, 104°E) p. 25

Slovenia (sloh•VEE•nee•uh) A country in eastern Europe. (46°N, 15°E) p. 24

Snake River A river that begins in the Rocky Mountains and flows west into the Pacific Ocean; part of the Oregon Trail ran along this river. p. 50

Sofia The capital city of Bulgaria. (43°N, 23°E) p. 24

Somalia A country in East Africa; formerly British Somaliland and Italian Somaliland. p. 22

Sonoran Desert (soh•NOHR•ahn) A part of the North American Desert, located in southwestern Arizona. p. 50

South Africa A country located in the southern tip of Africa, between the Atlantic and Indian oceans. p. 22

South America One of the world's seven continents. p. 18

South China Sea The part of the China Sea south of Taiwan. p. 21

South Korea A country in eastern Asia. p. 25

South Pole The southernmost point on the Earth. (90°S) p. 21

Southeast Region One of the five regions of the United States. p. 65

Spain A country in southwestern Europe, on the Iberian Peninsula. p. 24

Spokane (spoh•KAN) A city in eastern Washington on the falls of the Spokane River. (48°N, 117°W) p. 83

Springfield A city in southwestern Massachusetts; located on the Connecticut River, north of the Connecticut-Massachusetts border. (42°N, 73°W) p. 67

Springfield The capital of Illinois. (40°N, 90°W) p. 75

Sri Lanka An island country in South Asia, once known as Ceylon; located in the Indian Ocean west of India. (8°N, 81°E) p. 24

St. Augustine (AW•guh•steen) A city in Florida on the Atlantic Ocean; the oldest city founded by Europeans in the United States. (30°N, 81°W) p. 71

St. Croix (KROY) An island in the Caribbean Sea; the largest of the Virgin Islands. p. 72

St. John's A city on the southeastern coast of Canada, on the Atlantic Ocean; the capital of Newfoundland. (47°N, 52°W) p. 30

St. John An island in the Caribbean Sea; one of the Virgin Islands. p. 72

St. Lawrence River A river in northeastern North America; begins at Lake Ontario and flows into the Atlantic Ocean; forms part of the border between the United States and Canada. p. 30

St. Louis The largest city in Missouri; a major Mississippi River port; known as the Gateway to the West. (38°N, 90°W) p. 75

St. Paul The capital of Minnesota. (45°N, 93°W) p. 75

St. Petersburg A city formerly known as Leningrad when it served as the capital of the Russian empire; located on the Neva River on the Gulf of Finland. (60°N, 30°E) p. 24

St. Thomas An island in the Caribbean Sea; one of the Virgin Islands. p. 72

Stockholm The largest city in Sweden; located on the Baltic Sea. (59°N, 18°E) p. 24

Strait of Magellan (mah•JEH•lahn) The narrow waterway between the southern tip of South America and Tierra del Fuego; links the Atlantic Ocean with the Pacific Ocean. p. 20

Sucre A city in Bolivia, South America. (19°S, 65°W) p. 28

Sudan A country on the eastern coast of North Africa. p. 22

Suez Canal A canal linking the Mediterranean Sea and the Gulf of Suez; located in northeastern Egypt. p. 23

Sumatra (su•MAH•truh) The westernmost island of Indonesia; located off the Malay Peninsula in Southeast Asia. (40°N, 0°) p. 27

Suriname A country in north-central South America. p. 28

Susquehanna River (suhs•kwuh•HA•nuh) A river in Maryland, Pennsylvania, and central New York; rises in Otsego Lake, New York, and empties into northern Chesapeake Bay. p. 67

Swaziland A country in southern Africa. p. 22

Sweden A European country on the southeastern part of the Scandinavian Peninsula. p. 24

Switzerland A country in central Europe. p. 24

Syracuse A city in upper New York State. (43°N, 76°W) p. 67

Syria A country located on the eastern coast of the Mediterranean Sea. p. 24

Syrian Desert A desert covering southern Syria, northeast Jordan, western Iraq, and northern Saudi Arabia in Southwest Asia. p. 26

T

Taiwan (ty•WAHN) An island country; located off the southeastern coast of China. p. 25

Tajikistan (tah•jihk•ih•STAN) A country in western Asia; formerly part of the Soviet Union. p. 24

Takla Makan A desert in northwestern China. p. 26

Tallahassee (tal•uh•HA•see) The capital of Florida. (30°N, 84°W) p. 71

Tallinn The capital of the country of Estonia. (60°N, 25°E) p. 24

Tampa A city in western Florida; located on the northeastern end of Tampa Bay. (28°N, 82°W) p. 71

Tanzania A country in East Africa. p. 22

Tashkent The capital of Uzbekistan; located in western Asia. (41°N, 69°E) p. 24

Taurus Mountains A mountain range in southern Turkey; runs parallel to the southern Mediterranean coast and forms the border between Turkey and Syria. p. 26

Tegucigalpa A city in Central America; capital of Honduras. (14°N, 87°W) p. 28

Tennessee River A tributary of the Mississippi River; begins in eastern Tennessee and flows into the Ohio River in Kentucky. p. 71

Tenochtitlán (tay•nohch•teet•LAHN) An ancient settlement of the Aztec civilization; became the major center of Aztec trade and culture; located at the site of present-day Mexico City. (19°N, 99°W) p. 39

Thailand A country formerly known as Siam; located in Southeast Asia on the Indochina and Malay peninsulas. p. 25

Thar Desert Also called the Great Indian Desert; located in India and Pakistan. p. 26

Thimphu A city in central Bhutan; located north of western India. (28°N, 90°E) p. 25

Thunder Bay A city in southwestern Ontario, Canada; located on the shore of Lake Superior. (48°N, 89°W) p. 28

Tian Shan A mountain system in central Asia; extends northeast from the Pamirs into Xinjiang Uygur. p. 26

Tigris River A river in Southwest Asia; begins in eastern Turkey and joins the Euphrates River. p. 26

Tijuana (tee•WAH•nah) A city in northwestern Mexico. (33°N, 117°W) p. 31

Timbuktu (tim•buhk•TOO) An ancient Songhay trading center and present-day city; located in Mali on the Sahara, north of the Niger River. (17°N, 3°W) p. 39

Timor An island in Indonesia; formerly belonged to Portugal. (9°S, 125°E) p. 27

Tiranë The capital of Albania, located east of Durrës. (41°N, 20°E) p. 24

Tokyo The capital of Japan. (36°N, 140°E) p. 25

Toledo (tuh•LEE•doh) An industrial city and port; located in northwestern Ohio on the Maumee River at the southwest corner of Lake Erie. (42°N, 84°W) p. 75

Topeka (tuh•PEE•kuh) The capital of Kansas. (39°N, 96°W) p. 75

Toronto The capital of the province of Ontario, in Canada; located near the northwestern end of Lake Ontario; third-largest city in Canada. (43°N, 79°W) p. 28

Trenton The capital of New Jersey; site of an important battle in the American Revolution. (40°N, 75°W) p. 67

Trinidad and Tobago An independent state made up of the islands of Trinidad and Tobago; located in the Atlantic Ocean off the northeastern coast of Venezuela. p. 33

Tripoli The ancient Phoenician city of Oea and present-day capital of Libya. (33°N, 13°E) p. 22

Tropic of Cancer The line of latitude at 23½°N. pp. 20 and 21

Tropic of Capricorn The line of latitude at 23½°S. pp. 20 and 21

Tucson (TOO•sahn) A city in southeastern Arizona; located on the Santa Cruz River. (32°N, 111°W) p. 79

Tulsa (TUHL•suh) A city in Oklahoma. (36°N, 96°W) p. 79

Tunis The capital of Tunisia. p. 22

Tunisia A country in North Africa. p. 22

Turkey A country formerly known as Thrace; located mostly in northern Southwest Asia. p. 24

Turkmenistan (terk•mehn•uh•STAN) A country in western Asia; formerly part of the Soviet Union. p. 24

Tyrrhenian Sea (tuh•REE•nee•uhn) The sea located west of the Italian Peninsula, north of Sicily, and east of Sardinia and Corsica. p. 26

U

Uganda A country in East Africa; formerly part of British East Africa. p. 22

Ukraine (yoo•KRAYN) A country in eastern Europe; formerly part of the Soviet Union. p. 24

United Arab Emirates A country on the eastern Arabian Peninsula. p. 24

United Kingdom A European country made up of four kingdoms on the British Isles: England, Scotland, Wales, and northern Ireland. p. 24

United States A country in North America; a federal republic of fifty states. p. 18

Ural Mountains (YOOR•uhl) A mountain range in Russia and Kazakhstan; extends from the coast of the Arctic Ocean and borders part of Europe and Asia. p. 26

Ural River A river in Russia and Kazakhstan. p. 26

Uruguay A country on the Atlantic coast of southern South America. p. 28

Uzbekistan (uz•behk•ih•STAN) A country in western Asia; formerly part of the Soviet Union. p. 24

Valdivia A city located in the Los Lagos region in southern central Chile, on the Valdivia River. (39°S, 73°W) p. 28

Valencia A city on the Turia River, near the eastern coast of Spain. (39°N, 0°) p. 24

Valparaíso A seaport located in Chile, west northwest of Santiago on the Bay of Valparaíso; capital of Valparaíso. (33°S, 71°W) p. 28

Vancouver Canada's eighth-largest city; located where the north arm of the Fraser River empties into the Pacific Ocean. (49°N, 123°W) p. 30

Vancouver Island An island off the southwest coast of British Columbia, Canada. p. 30

Venezuela A country in northern South America; former territory of Spain. (8°N, 66°W) p. 28

Veracruz (veh•rah•KROOZ) A seaport in eastern Mexico; located on the Gulf of Mexico. (19°N, 96°W) p. 28

Victoria Falls The Zambezi River waterfall; located between Zimbabwe and Zambia, in central Africa. (18°S, 26°E) p. 23

Victoria Island The third largest of Canada's Arctic Islands. p. 29

Vienna The capital city of Austria in Europe; located in northeastern Austria, on the Danube River. (48°N, 16°E) p. 24

Vientiane An administrative capital of Laos. (18°N, 103°E) p. 25

Vietnam A country in Southeast Asia; located on the Indochina Peninsula. p. 25

Vilnius The capital of Lithuania. (55°N, 25°E) p. 24

Virgin Islands A group of islands between the Caribbean Sea and the Atlantic Ocean that are United States territories. p. 72

Virginia Beach A city and ocean resort in Virginia. (37°N, 76°W) p. 71

Volga River (VAHL•guh) A river in Russia; the longest river in Europe. p. 26

Voyageurs National Park A national park in northern Minnesota. p. 75

Wabash River (WAW•bash) A river that flows west and southwest across Indiana to form part of the Indiana–Illinois border. p. 75

Warsaw The capital of Poland. (52°N, 21°E) p. 24

Washington, D.C. The capital of the United States; located on the Potomac River in a special district that is not part of any state. (39°N, 77°W) p. 67

West Region One of the five regions of the United States. p. 64

Western Ghats A chain of mountains in southwestern India. p. 26

Western Sahara A former Spanish province; located in northwestern Africa. p. 22

Wheeler Peak A mountain in New Mexico. (36°N, 105°W) p. 79

White Mountains A mountain range in northern New Hampshire. p. 67

Whitehorse The capital of the Yukon Territory, Canada; located on the south bank of the Yukon River. (60°N, 135°W) p. 30

Wichita (WIH•chuh•taw) A city in Kansas. (37°N, 97°W) p. 75

Williamsburg A city in southeastern Virginia; located on a peninsula between the James and York rivers. (37°N, 77°W) p. 58

Wilmington A city in North Carolina. (34°N, 78°W) p. 71

Wind Cave National Park A national park in southwestern South Dakota. p. 75

Winnipeg The capital of the province of Manitoba, in Canada; located on the Red River; fourth-largest city in Canada. (50°N, 97°W) p. 30

Wisconsin River A river that flows south through central Wisconsin, turns west, and then enters the Mississippi River on the border between Crawford and Grant counties. p. 75

Xian (shee•ahn) A city in eastern China; also known as Sian; formerly Chang'an. (34°N, 109°E) p. 25

Y

Yangoon See Rangoon.

Yellow Sea The sea south of the Korean Peninsula and east of China. p. 27

Yellowknife A town in southern Mackenzie district, Canada; located on the northwestern shore of Great Slave Lake at the mouth of the Yellowknife River; capital of the Northwest Territories. (62°N, 114°W) p. 30

Yellowstone River A river in northwestern Wyoming and southern and eastern Montana. pp. 50 and 51

Yucatán Peninsula (yoo•kah•TAN) A peninsula in southeastern Mexico and northern Central America. p. 29

Yukon River (YOO•kahn) A river that begins in the southwestern Yukon Territory, Canada, flows through Alaska, and empties into the Bering Sea. p. 29

Yukon Territory One of Canada's three territories. p. 30

Yuma (YOO•muh) A city in southwestern Arizona. (33°N, 115°W) p. 79

Z

Zagros Mountains A mountain range; located in western and southern Iran. p. 26

Zambezi River A river in southern Africa; flows from northwestern Zambia to the Indian Ocean. p. 23

Zambia A country in southern Africa. p. 22

Zimbabwe A country in southern Africa. p. 22